Is *THAT* what they meant?

A book of practical communication insights

by Robert J. Rubel, Ph.D.
with
M. Jen Fairfield

Is *THAT* what they meant?

A book of practical communication insights

by Robert J. Rubel, Ph.D.
with
M. Jen Fairfield

Red Eight Ball Press
P.O. Box 171303
Austin, TX 78717

Red Eight Ball Press
P.O. Box 171303 Austin, TX 78717

Is THAT what they meant?
A book of practical communication insights

Layout: I particularly wish to recognize and thank s. kitara for the
exceptional job she did laying out this book.

Library of Congress Control Number: 2016949539

Published by Red Eight Ball Press
Printed in the United States of America

Dedication

This book is dedicated to those of you who have the personal courage to seek resources to help you to strengthen your relationship. My hat is off to you. This is a path for those who understand they must work on themselves in order to improve the way they interact with others. This is a book about taking personal responsibility for your communication. This is a path for couples who are seeking more harmony in their relationship.

We hope that this book adds tools to your relationship toolbox. That is certainly our intent.

Foreword

Once upon a time, on a lovely Spring afternoon, I was reading a book while curled up on the living room sofa. My then-partner came in and observed that we were having a particularly beautiful day. I looked up from my book, turned and looked out the window. "Yes," I agreed. "It's a lovey day." I returned to reading my book and she walked out of the room.

She reentered the room about ten minutes later and again pointed out that the day was just so beautiful... I put down the book and looked out of the window. Again, I agreed: the day was really beautiful. She walked back out of the room.

I suppose that another ten minutes passed before she returned. This time her face expressed hurt/upset. "Why won't you go for a walk with me?" she demanded.

More astonished than annoyed at the third interruption, I said that I'd be glad to go for a walk with her, but that she hadn't asked. "I've asked you twice within the last fifteen minutes," she replied.

Clearly, we had a communications upset.

≠≠≠≠≠≠≠≠≠≠≠≠≠≠≠≠≠≠≠≠≠≠≠≠≠≠≠≠≠≠≠≠≠

There are two primary reasons for this book.

First, while there are many communication resource books, most of them present a particular viewpoint or skill. I wanted to approach the subject more broadly and refer you to places to find greater detail.

Second, over the years I've observed that communication difficulties often stem from differences in communication styles and personal upbringings. Let me offer two comparisons: The way a litigating criminal attorney is taught to think and speak differs from how a civil contracts lawyer is taught to think and speak. Their jobs require different communication skills. Similarly, the social customs and communication styles differ between someone brought up in a small New England town versus someone raised as a Southern Belle in a small Southern town.

All relationships have bumps and wrinkles. One person prefers taking vacations near water, and the other partner doesn't like being out in the sun. Most individual differences fall within tolerated boundaries, but some push against those boundaries and are expressed as upsets. While most upsets have fairly obvious roots, others can be puzzling or confusing. Misunderstandings can arise because people think slightly differently; it is often difficult to identify the thought differences that led to the upset.

Also, some of the variables that make us who we are as adults are largely invisible to us because they're accepted and supported by our culture. It doesn't occur to us to question our own (or our partner's) basic assumptions about who we are and how we interact in the world. It's difficult to step aside from yourself and explore why you think as you do.

Hence this book.

This book is designed to bring up a lot of topics in a general way so that you'll have areas to explore more deeply when you feel that they've hit a sensitive nerve. I hope the book will help you improve the communication in your relationships.

Best wishes,
Bob Rubel and M. Jen Fairfield
Austin, Texas 2016

Contents

On Relationship as Vocation
By G. E. Martt

People pursue many careers, many passions - many do so
without any specific plan while others pursue them
with a concerted effort. Diligence. Strategy. Goals.
What if we sought Relationships with such dedication?

Imagine creating a résumé for a Relationship position, listing
all of the skills and experiences that might qualify you for
the position you hope to secure? Attributes. Experience.
Training. References. Contact information.

Imagine applying for a Relationship for the purpose of learning
what duties would be expected, and how it would be rewarded.
Imagine the interview process - what would you say?
How would you offer yourself to another?

Imagine having a Relationship based on this understanding,
one with clear expectations and requirements, one which
would continue as long as the criteria was met, or be
terminated if one's performance was unsatisfactory?

We seek meaning in our lives. We seek expression.
We seek gainful employment and a place to live.
We seek nourishment and enjoyable experiences.
What if Relationships embodied what we seek?

Chapter One
Getting on the Same Page

"As your partner, in order to know what to do when you are with me I have to respect who you are without me."

Karen Martin

Orientation

The famous psychiatrist Carl Jung once wrote that, "The meeting of two personalities is like the contact of two chemical substances: if there is any reaction, both are transformed." (*Modern Man in Search of a Soul* by Carl Jung, 1933, page 49.)

In order for Jung's two personalities to meet, they must speak, or risk bypassing one another in the flow of their individual busyness. Before speaking, people (nearly instantly) run through available strategic options for saying something—*anything*.

In order to select an appropriate communication technique, it's useful to have a range of techniques available in your communications toolbox. You can help your brain build communication skills. To do that, you at least have to realize that there are skills out there that you don't yet know. This book will expose you to some communication techniques that may be new to you. You'll have to practice them in order to be able to use them when needed.

This book offers a little bit of information about a lot of communication and relationship topics. I hope you will research those that interest you. This material is heavily pragmatic and you can use most of these techniques and insights immediately; however, some of the communication concepts in here require thought and practice. For example, we'll spend quite a bit of time discussing how people take in information and communicate their wants and needs. Your challenge is to learn to discern how others think in order to build rapport when you speak with them.

While communication suggestions in this book apply generally to all settings, I've focused on partnership communication. I did done this because the success of your home life depends largely on the ability the two of you have to speak together successfully. When you're happy in your home life, you have a better shot at being happy in your work life.

Because I can't know how much you know about communication theories and practices, it is likely that you'll know some of this material. However, we expect that at least one or two ideas will not have occurred to you and will be useful.

My main theme is that adults have unique backgrounds. As we form our lives, we have preconceptions of how things are. Our socio-economic status, upbringing, and education level governs these perceptions. Even if you grew up across the street from your partner, the way your respective parents raised you (and the differences in your life experiences) affect how each of you now listen, process what you hear, and respond to one another.

Your unique backgrounds lead to unique communication styles. While most people generally understand others speaking in a common language, in intimate settings—in relationships—miscues can be subtle and can build up over time. I know of many cases where one person has created a very different version of their partner than that person would describe.

Communication becomes much more challenging when people come from different cultures, even within the US. Clearly, the cultural upbringing of someone whose parents were hippies differs profoundly from someone whose parents were outlaw bikers, New England fishermen, or medical doctors. The way each of you has learned to respond to others is a direct outgrowth of how you learned to handle easy and confrontational situations as a child.

We've all had times when communication went smoothly and left us with good and lasting memories. We've also all had times when something went slightly wrong and left us with the sense that the message wasn't quite delivered the way it was intended. Most of us have also had unfortunate reactions to people or events that turned out to have long-term negative ramifications. For some of us, these memories gather together to hold hands and form a foundation of guilt, regret, and lowered self-image.

There are many books on communication theory and practice. I've read a selection of them. I have also taken a number of communication courses. Perhaps more to the point, I'm over 70, have written many relationship books, and lectured widely on relationship communication issues.

Of course, it's also helped that I've experienced several different communication styles from partners in my personal and business relationships and I had to learn quite a bit about communication in order to adapt to these situations.

I didn't come up with the ideas in this book; others thought of them, so I've blended and applied them. As you read, you'll see them pop up in all sorts of places. Some come from business management and negotiation guides, Neuro-Linguistic Programming (NLP) material, generic self-help books, and guides to various forms of therapy. I've taken what has seemed important and useful and now present them to you in what I hope is an interesting and useful fashion.

I spend quite a bit of time thinking, writing, and speaking about relationship communication. But remember: a "relationship" can be a work relationship or a personal relationship. It's all about the communication.

I write in the first-person present tense: I'm speaking directly to you. Just consider this book to be a short personal visit. In addition, I lecture and write in spirals. I'll introduce a topic lightly at first, then bring it in again with a little more detail, then discuss it in much more depth a third time. I do this in order to build up your knowledge around that topic: by the time you're exposed to the detailed discussion, the ideas sound familiar.

Why This Book May Interest You

Permit me to frame some reasons why this book might interest you.

- **It's almost working, but...** You sense that you're missing something—you're no longer building to the initial vision. In the beginning, it was clear what you both wanted, but as the new relationship energy faded, something became lost. You keep trying to speak about it, but you're not connecting emotionally as you would need for serious discussions.

- **You've lost track of the goal.** One or the other of you had a general idea where you wanted to go (how you wanted to be) as a couple, but the vision never quite jelled. You each entered the relationship with different skills and knowledge, yet as your lives settled and became busy, you stopped working toward anything in particular. You keep trying to talk about it, but you're not quite connecting as you would like to.

- **You're looking for The Real Deal, whatever that may be.** You've had trouble establishing or keeping a relationship. *Stuff* happens. It's different with different people, but you're finding it hard to maintain the relationship. You're hoping to find new ideas you can apply personally with your partner, hence your interest in this book.

- **You'd like to intensify your relationship.** It's not that there is anything exactly *wrong* with your relationship; it's just that there is nothing spectacularly *right* about it.

This book is about exposing you to a wide range of techniques that can change the way you interact with others in an effort to be more present with them. This book is about learning how to make your times together *magical* (whatever "magical" looks like to you).

Concepts to Consider

Russell Hoban once observed: "When you come right down to it, how many people speak the same language even when they speak the same language?" (*A Russell Hoban Omnibus* by Russell Hoban, 1998, p.130) When I first read that sentence many decades ago, I wondered... why is that so? The older I grew, the more sense it made.

For most of us, the way we speak and listen has resulted from survival reactions developed almost from the first days of our life. Your father/mother raised their voice(s) and you took that to mean something. They told you forcibly to be quiet and you, not realizing they were having an upset, reacted in your own world as though *you* had done something wrong. Human instincts taught you to build defenses. You may have learned to become very forceful or you may have learned to become very passive. It depends. But, over the years, you developed the personality you now have. As I alluded to in the opening paragraphs of this book, whether or not you're a good communicator flows from your childhood experiences combined with your upbringing.

Your upbringing and early adult experiences have played major roles in the way you are as an adult. Unless you have studied communications techniques and worked consciously to alter the way you listen to others and react to what they say, chances are that your current communication style is fundamentally the same as it was when you were 15 or so. Basically, this means that your early social conditioning is still with you. For example, the way you react to authority figures developed from the way you were permitted to react to your own parents' authority.

Your Relationship to Your World

We all have "viewpoints." We see the world in our own particular ways. Here are three of my own viewpoints that affect this book:

- **Things** are **visitors** in our lives. While we have many things around us, they don't define us. If they go, they go. If they break, they break. Visitors. People with this view tend to avoid getting upset when things break or are stolen. In a "woo" sense, they feel that whatever has left their lives was meant to do so. When you purposefully avoid putting energy into *things,* you have more energy to focus on the *people* who matter to you.

- **Relationships enrich people**; they expose you to new ideas and experiences. Relationships require care, particularly when it comes to communication. A wrong word here or there can drive people away from you.

- **Recurring patterns** can be changed. Only you are in charge of you. You've doubtless heard the saying: "If it's going to be, it's up to me." Well, nobody can hurt your feelings, it's all in your ability to control your emotional self and figure out how that particular button got pushed and why you cared.

These distinctions are important, as this book is really about examining your repetitive communication patterns. The truth is, our upbringing, education, and past life experiences strongly influence who we are. Who we are impacts all our relationships. Our relationships influence our self-image. Our self-image affects our professional success as well as the way we walk, speak, and dress in everyday life.

Knowing Yourself and Your Partner

This book dives deeply into core concepts that underpin a relationship and examines essential aspects of ways you think about and react to people. This book is cerebral; there's no point apologizing for it. Life is complex, and it takes some work to explore the nooks and crannies of this subject to find where sociologists and psychologists have hidden the clues.

One of my core messages is that "Our reality is influenced by our notions about reality, regardless of the nature of those notions." [*The Crack in the Cosmic Egg: New Constructs of Mind and Reality* by Joseph Chilton Pearce. Revised Edition, 2002] Joseph Chilton Pearce] That means that to the extent that one develops a point of view (a reality) that differs from our partner's point of view, the danger increases that our core assumptions about many things will not align well with that partner. Down that path lives conflict.

Another core message is that "Your reality is built on the sands of your assumptions." (See: *How to Give and Receive Advice* by Gerald Nirenberg, 1975.) That is, your current personality has been built upon wide-ranging assumptions about what is right and wrong, good and evil, safe and harmful, etc. Actually, each of our assumptions evolved from a survival reaction to personal experiences. When you were very young, something happens that you don't understand (because you're so young). You (as an infant) decide, "Well, I didn't like what just happened, but if I do Y in the future, maybe X won't happen to me again." Thousands upon thousands of tiny decisions have formed the *"you"* that you are today.

Most of us are blind to why we act as we do. We are blind to how we got the way we are. By extraction, this means that unless one or both of you are particularly insightful, neither quite understands why you do things as you do them, and why many of your daily conflicts/discomforts arise in the first place. That's a problem.

It's a problem, because one or the other (or both) of you is likely to react in ways that don't quite make sense to the other person. That is why so much of this book is devoted to helping you to uncover hidden assumptions or hidden expectations.

MUCH of this book focuses on concepts and assumptions. A smaller portion of this book addresses ways you can fix the problem(s). This is very purposeful. In my experience, many challenging relationship situations get named *problems* because you can't quite figure out what went wrong. You can't quite name it one thing or another, so you come to look at it as a problem. Chances are if you *could* name the underlying cause of what went wrong, you'd be able to solve it.

I've interspersed some aphorisms (proverbs) throughout this book. They have a way of summarizing great wisdom. For example, take the saying: "If you don't have what you want, you are not 100% committed to it." This is particularly relevant at this point in the book, for if you intend to get what you want by being 100% committed to it, you'll have to commit to speaking with your partner at a new level of clarity. Fresh communication skills can help to clean out the cobwebs of misunderstanding and misinterpretation that have grown up to affect your interactions.

And that's a good place to leave this first chapter.

Relationship Issues

There are serious and tangible consequences to communication failure within a relationship, yet people seldom discuss their relationship's basic structure. Common archetypes of boyfriend/girlfriend or husband/wife are so prevalent/strong that few people consider other options. And there are options.

Just sticking with a male/female pairing for a moment, the prevalent structure has the man making the long-range decisions according to his vision of the relationship. Sometimes that works, sometimes it doesn't work. There are many men who prefer letting the woman lead and have strong and successful bonds. How do I know? Because I am one of them and I'm part of a culture that supports female-led partnerships. I'm not saying that one is better than the other or easier than the other, only that relationships can suffer from one partner not letting the more skillful leader take charge.

Whether male- or female-led, there are options available within your relationship structure. Some people who lead the relationship are most comfortable taking a hierarchical role: what they want is the way it's going to be. Balancing that, other relationships stress a team-model role: the leader helps their partner realize their potential. Beyond that, your own preferences (should) govern the operational mechanics of the relationship. Who makes certain kinds of decisions, who needs to be consulted for purchases over a certain amount, who drives the car, and so forth.

Now, let's go on to another structure. One hears about one partner "cheating" on the other. Feelings are hurt. Divorces keep lawyers in business. However, some couples—particularly those who have great communication skills—have managed to live with more than one significant other. In many cultures, it's the norm rather than the exception. Yes, I understand that the Western culture only endorses monogamy, but I also understand that one or both partners in many relationships go through HUGE emotional angst, upset, and trauma when infidelity is revealed. You sidestep infidelity by discussing your planned outside relationships. (Note: read about polyamory if you're considering this path.)

So: back to communication.

To a large extent, options available for solving communication challenges depend on the relationship's authority structure. That is, if the follower has given the leader a great deal of authority for making decisions and guiding the relationship, the leader (of either gender) can (essentially) require their follower to behave as instructed.

When that kind of authority is applied to communication topics, the recognized leader can require their partner to speak in certain ways or to react to situations according to some procedure (protocol) they've designed. On the other hand, if the two people have essentially equal authority, they must both agree that some approach or strategy is okay to use.

Parenthetically, that's why authority-heavy structures such as the Military or a religious order can accomplish so much so quickly: when the person with authority says to jump, people jump.

Authority

You're living together or thinking about it. If you're a man brought up in the US, you assume that you're going to lead the relationship. If you're a woman brought up in the US, you may be a little conflicted. You realize that public support for the "1950s housewife" relationship model has faded away, but so has the "get a career" push of the 1970s and 80s. You know you're pretty dominant in most aspects of your life, but submissive in others. You're willing to give your partner a certain amount of leadership leeway, but you have limits. You're not quite sure what those limits are, but you have them.

Life is about give and take: you help someone; someone helps you. Some couples believe that relationships are also about give and take: they share decision-making roles based on a partner's particular strengths and experiences. Other couples have structured their relationship so one person makes all the significant decisions without discussing them with their partner.

I'm not suggesting one is better than the other. I'm only asking you to take a moment to be honest with yourself about where you and your partner stand on the *leader/follower* scale, and then think about the *nature* of your exchange. This is relevant, because you may not be able to get your partner to participate in some of the suggestions listed throughout this book: they may resist you simply because of their understanding of their role within the relationship.

This issue of resistance may also apply if you have children: *they* may not appreciate parental coaching on this subject.

Just a thought.

Coordinating communication strategies with two people requires real leadership and serious, thoughtful (and sometimes painful) discussions. These discussions are necessary because each of you has somewhat different mental images (expectations) about what, exactly, your relationship is supposed to be. Expectations may have come from the Internet, from books, from TV, or from seeing other couples who appear to look so fulfilled. Particularly for females, preconceptions may originate from seeds planted in bodice-ripper novels; some preconceptions doubtlessly come simply from some women's wishes to be totally taken care of and loved. On the men's part, misconceptions seem to arise over the fantasy of playing the hero in a scene and living it in real-time.

Motivations

I want to touch on some motivations underlying your relationship before we start describing communication strategies. Here, I'd like you to consider what motivates you to live together. Here are some options (we'll discuss this in greater depth later in the book):

- **Love**. Your union is based on love. You work hard to make sure that your actions support your love for your partner. This is *eros*: Aristotle's term for romantic love.

- **Service (Nurturing)**. You love giving (or receiving) service and you're gratified in your relationship so long as you feel you're providing (or receiving) outstanding service. The person serving is providing time for the person being served to perform activities that are supported by the person serving. In some ways, you believe you're serving a *higher calling* of some kind.

Aristotle called this *agape*. Essentially, this is "love by choice." Some call it spiritual love.

- **Friendship**. For many, love changes to intimate friendship after the "new relationship energy" phase wears off. "*Philia*" is Aristotle's term for *brotherly love*.

There is another reason some people choose to remain together even when love, service, and friendship have failed: it's simply the pragmatic thing to do. Often a person will remain longer after they should because of money, minor children, or a sense of duty.

Obviously, the look and feel of your own relationship represents a blend of these basic motivations. A little too much of one or too little of another can produce a result that you feel is a little "off" somehow. Relationship misunderstandings and miscommunication often originate from mismatched relationship motivations.

Here is an example of a motivation mismatch: Two people are going out on a date. One person is deeply in love with the other. However, the "other" views this is a "friendship date"—they're not interested in falling in love right now. If love is primarily motivating one person but friendship is primarily motivating the other person, the evening's outcome probably won't meet either person's expectations. Each person is reaching out to connect with the other and not getting back the expected signals. One person is trying to connect emotionally/romantically while the other person is trying to keep the relationship toned down to friendship and is getting tired of fighting off their date's emotional outreach.

What am I getting at? Reading about communication tips and techniques will only get you so far. Successful application depends to a large extent upon whether your partner also believes that improved communication will improve your relationship—and they actually *want* to improve the relationship! Successful application also requires that the two (or more) of you are similarly motivated. Said another way, do you have the same relationship purpose and desire to maintain that purpose?

Risks

If you're not working on your relationship, you're really not *in* the relationship. That applies to each of you.

How you handle the care and nurturing of your relationship largely depends on how the relationship is structured. The way the relationship is structured will affect (or control) the ways each of you deals with *upsets.*

That said, you may have to sit down and write out who has authority over what and ensure that you have common relationship motivations and a shared vision of the future. You may also wish to write out an agreement about how you will work through upsets and challenges with honor and integrity.

You'll want to have a set plan for sharing intimate feelings in a safe setting. This sentence is important, because people who feel unsafe in a personal relationship will be guarded and unforthcoming. To feel safe sharing information, consider a rule that nothing said by either of you can be used against the other person. Also, to ensure emotional safety, the other person must not react emotionally to what you say.

Relationships are tough, and good communication skills are certainly important. Here are some other important communication considerations relevant for home or work settings.

- **Point of focus.** If someone shows you a white piece of paper with a red dot on it and asks you what you see, most people will say: "A red dot on a piece of white paper." That's natural; they're focusing on the anomaly, on what is unusual about that piece of paper. Relationships have a similar risk. If one partner finds certain displeasing behaviors in the other partner, they may get distracted from looking at the good parts of the relationship and focus on parts that aren't working so well. "Red dot behavior" is the tendency to focus on the parts rather than the whole. Worse, the better the overall relationship is working, the greater the tendency to notice the few things that **aren't** working. Obviously, it's a constant battle to overcome this characteristic of human nature.

- **Participant observer bias.** Both you and your partner will experience behavioral changes as a function of the work you each put into such change. Those changes will prompt other changes; it's a dynamic process. In order to change the way the two of you relate to, you both are going to have to work on *yourselves*. Fortunately, the amount and quality of this work depends upon your abilities to communicate—back to why you bought this book.

- **Focus and intent.** Focus and intent can alter the way you react to the world. There are techniques for replacing negative thoughts with positive thoughts and slowing or softening your "inner voice." Your ability to be here, now, and with your partner is improved when you are saying good things to yourself about yourself.

What You Think You Know

We're going to take a quick look at three relevant topics:

- The Johari Window
- Visible and invisible knowledge
- Conscious and unconscious knowledge

The Johari Window

The Johari Window is a tool for illustrating and improving not only your self-awareness, but also awareness and understanding between you and others close to you. Rather than measuring personality, the Window presents a way of looking at how personality is expressed—a good topic for this communications book.

This process is not introspective; it requires interaction and feedback. Let me start with a brief overview of the Johari Window.

	Known by self	NOT known by self
Known by others	Square 1: The public area	Square 2: The blind spot
NOT known by others	Square 3: The hidden area	Square 4: The unknown area

Square 1: The open (public) area contains information about you that is openly known and spoken about by yourself and others. This area includes aspects of your strengths or weaknesses that you and others know about. It contains information about your behavior, attitude, feelings, emotion, knowledge, experience, skills, views, and so forth. Together, these make up your known self.

Square 2: The blind area or blind spot contains the information that you don't know about yourself, *but that others know about you.* (A scary thought. I highly recommend the book if you're interested in learning how to start seeing yourself as others see you. *Leadership and Self-Deception: Getting out of the box* by The Arbinger Institute, 2010. It's written like a story you would tell your child, but it packs a big punch.)

Square 3: The hidden area holds your secret stuff. Secret stuff is what you know about yourself that you try to keep from others. This is also called the area of the hidden self, the avoided area, or the avoided self. People often become reactive to others they see exhibiting behaviors you particularly dislike in yourself. Next time you find yourself getting angry and someone, consider stopping and considering the source of your anger. Are *they* doing something you work very hard not to do?

Square 4: The unknown area or unknown self is made up of everything about yourself that is not only unknown by you, but also unknown by others. If you go to a psychiatrist, this is where they like to hang out. By the way, because you don't know what you don't know, you don't know that you can gain control of this hidden material and change your core reactions to the world around you. Also, there are two substantial barriers keeping you from discovering this "unknown area." First, it takes a lot of time, coaching, and concentration to work in this area; second, the hard work is made harder because the doorkeeper's name is "Denial."

Anyway, I'll get back on topic.

The general goal when working with a Johari Window is to open up the public area and make the other three areas as small as possible. That is, you're trying to expose or uncover information about yourself that you've kept private or you haven't previously owned up to. This can be done by reading books that help you figure yourself out, by journaling, through specific coursework (such as the Landmark Education Forum), or by using a professional counselor (counselor, psychologist, or psychiatrist, depending on credentialing).

NOTE: If you're thinking of opening yourself up to your partner, I suggest you keep it simple: the goal is to help them understand what you find easy and difficult in order to be able to provide appropriate support.

Fundamentally, the "you" that you know is comprised of certain strengths. You can make a list of them. However, once you name some of these attributes, you realize that virtually every other personal characteristic that you did *not* name contains some hidden truth about you that can be discovered through interaction/feedback from others. An Internet search will give you lots of information about and examples of Johari Windows. They're versatile; they have multiple applications.

Within the relationship, this instrument may be useful to help you and your partner to find discussion points to begin mutual introspection. To the extent that communication barriers break down between you, the two or more of you will become transparent to one another.

Transparent means that neither of you has significant weaknesses (discomfort zones) or preference that are being withheld from the other. To the extent that you hide information from your partner, you are controlled by that secret and your relationship will suffer in some way. This occurs because you have to put energy into hiding/disguising some trait that you don't like in yourself, or that you are afraid that your partner will reject. The more work you're putting into this kind of defensive action, the less you can be present with others, including your partner.

For some people, being open and transparent is easier said than done. People vary in the degrees of openness and sharing they will permit, even with someone with whom they've lived for decades. Also, people have different levels of self-awareness: some of your more perspective friends may know more profound things about you than you do. Another scary thought.

So, the more you and your partner explore topics such as fears, fantasies, preferences, and avoidances, the more your *open area* will expand. This *open area* is the space where good communications and cooperation occur, free from distractions, mistrust, confusion, conflict, and misunderstanding. This open area is the easiest to work on, as it's so heavily influenced by such subjective attributes as behavior, empathy, cooperation, inter-personal development, and so forth.

Visible and Invisible Knowledge

This topic is actually quite different from the Johari discussion of *open* and *blind* information. Johari is dealing with openness between people; this section tackles the cause of misunderstandings between people because one of the two doesn't have the same background knowledge as the other. The listener *thinks* they got the message, but they didn't.

Each of you has knowledge that is *invisible* to your partner. Some quick examples:

- **Business practices.** You may not have the same knowledge about business practices:

    ○ You may want your partner to use a business planning approach for a new project for the two of you. This doesn't work out because the world of project performance, feedback loops, risk analysis, and system dynamics are unknown to them.

    ○ You ask that your partner change the routing on an overnight delivery of three packages. The process fails because you assumed your partner knew to specifically confirm the rerouting information for each piece when multiple packages are involved.

- **Interpersonal skills.** You may not have the same knowledge about working with people:

    ○ You notice that your partner is a little "off" when around other people. Finally, you realize that your partner has worked alone through most of their prior jobs and only rudimentary socializing skills.

- You notice that your partner becomes reactive in stressful situations. Discussing this with them reveals they have no training in coping with difficult conversations and are relying solely on personal experiences.

- **Upbringing.** You may not have the same background due to gender differences resulting from being brought up within the Western culture:

  - Ladies: you may not know which tools you'd need to do a plumbing repair.

  - Guys: you may not know how to iron a shirt or cook a good meal. Actually, you may not know that there are "better" and "best" ways to sweep the floor with a broom.

Not only are there gender-linked areas of blindness resulting from how boys and girls are socialized, but there are knowledge and experience gaps between social classes. For example, one of you may have been brought up with extensive international travel that has led to a more tolerant view of people than the other person expresses. One of you may have grown up in a small town in the heartland of America and have much clearer moral and ethical positions than your partner who grew up in one of the 10 largest cities in the country.

Message: Your gender, upbringing, education, and work experiences all conspire to give you and your partner slightly different views of the same topic/issue. Communication gaps between people are closed as you tease out and discuss these differences.

If you'd like a little diversion, here's an exercise you can do with your partner. Write out your "worldview." A worldview is a theory of the world, used for living in the world, it describes how your most basic beliefs play out in your life. You can work this project from the inside out or from the outside in. You can start with worldview and end up describing behaviors or take a behavior and chisel it down to worldview.

If you think of a series of concentric circles, "worldview" is in the middle. Next come your beliefs (what is true for you), then your *values* (what is good or best), and finally your *behavior* (what is done).

You'll probably need some Internet help with this, but here is an example of a worldview. If you believe in karma, as millions do, how do you translate it into action in your own life? If you know of someone who is suffering and you have the power to help them, do you not help them because you think suffering is their karma? Or do you help them, because it is your karma?

This is not a make-work project. You'll learn a lot about one another. If you'll take some time to work this project to show how each of you perceives the world, the two or more of you can create a more harmonious future. By the way, I'm a huge fan of the Myers-Briggs assessment. We'll discuss it in depth in Chapter Three.

Conscious and Unconscious Knowledge

As I often point out, you have to be aware that an area of knowledge exists in order even to think about learning about it. After all, when you're a one-year-old, you don't know much more than that a few sounds that you make produce results that seem to satisfy you. You only have to consider how much you now know to appreciate how many ideas you've been exposed to throughout your life. But, did you ever stop to wonder *how* you learn new information? When starting a new job, have you ever considered how new skills or knowledge move from being invisible to you to being automatic for you?

The answer is that in a general way, there are four stages of developing competence in any field. Knowing about these four stages will help you to assess the amount of training you and/or your partner will need when you encounter a new idea.

- **Unconscious incompetence**. You don't know something, but you don't really know that you don't know it.

- **Conscious incompetence**. Though you don't understand some concept (or know how to do something), you recognize that some people *do* understand that thing (or know how to do it). Once you decide to learn something new, your learning involves making mistakes.

- **Conscious competence**. You understand or know how to do something, but demonstrating the skill or knowledge requires concentration. The new skill or knowledge may be broken down into steps, and you may have to focus on each step in order to do it. (Put the key in the car's ignition; turn the car on; check the rear-view mirror...)

- **Unconscious competence**. You have had so much practice with a skill that it has become second nature and you can perform it easily and without conscious thought. As a result, the skill can be performed while executing another task or two (e.g.: scrambling eggs while preparing coffee and watching the bacon all while listening to the radio). You have reached *understanding,* and you would now be able to teach that knowledge or skill to others.

Look: life in general involves a complex learning curve. The more you learn, the more you realize that there is a lot more to learn. Educated people have known this for eons. Here are the same concepts expressed elegantly as an ancient Oriental proverb:

He who knows not, and knows not that he knows not, is a fool; shun him.
(Unconscious Incompetent)

He who knows not, and knows that he knows not, is ignorant; teach him.
(Conscious Incompetent)

He who knows, and knows not that he knows, is asleep; wake him.
(Unconscious Competent)

He who knows, and knows that he knows, is a wise man; follow him.
(Conscious Competent)

One of life's many tasks is to increase your "correct knowledge" and reduce your "incorrect knowledge." Often, though, one is so sure they are right that it's hard for them to set ego aside and truly listen for ways to expand their correct knowledge.

Difficulties

The word "difficulty" means different things to different people in different situations. If someone says they're "having a difficult time" or "in a difficulty," we can guess about their problems, but we don't really know what they mean unless they offer explanations. Furthermore, expressions such as "having difficulties" or "having problems" can be a person's code meaning they're not happy with their emotional condition, but don't really want to talk about it.

Difficulties have different causes and different solutions depending upon their nature and your nature. What one person sees as a rather straightforward task may be viewed as *daunting* by another person. This section is meant to help demystify the concept of "difficulty."

Difficulties arise within relationships, actions, and communication. The point that triggers someone to think that a task is difficult usually falls into one of the following categories:

Luck Difficulty vs. Effort Difficulty: The first distinction is whether the difficulty is related to effort. If something is difficult but the outcome doesn't depend much on effort, then it must depend on luck. If you're having a difficult time putting a jigsaw puzzle together, there's not much you can do about it beyond sticking with it and looking harder for the correct shapes.

Luck difficulty and *effort* difficulty are often confused. Publishing a profitable book is difficult, but it's mostly effort difficulty. If you stick at it and continue to hone your writing and marketing skills, experience shows you're likely to succeed. It's about the same for learning a new language. Success is really determined by the amount of time you commit to the project.

Varieties of Luck: There are different kinds of "luck difficulty." Some luck happens only once: your physical size enables you to excel in some activity or sport, or you're born with some genetic gift and find yourself composing symphonies by age 5 like Mozart. Other types of luck continue over time. As you gain excellence in a field, luck may have been involved early in the process but become unnecessary. For example, you may find yourself at the right place at the right time with the right training. Voila! You're in luck. Benefits and rewards will follow you once you begin to gain recognition for your expert knowledge and skills. In situations where greater expertise pays greater rewards, the requirement for *luck* gives way to the requirement for *tenacity* (another word for *effort*).

Quantifying Difficulty: **Since you have to communicate to give someone an assignment, I'd like to spend some time discussing ways to approach asking someone to perform a task they see as difficult.**

Difficult assignments can be made easier by breaking them down into their component parts and putting parameters around each part. In the world of business, these are called "project management sheets" or "time-and-task sheets" or "milestone analyses." Once you write out all the steps and can see the actual scope of work, the task may appear less formidable.

You can build personal systems (often referred to as "protocols") to manage projects. Here is a pragmatic example. This is the "protocol" that I've used for years concerning agreements. It works with adults and with children.

Agreements have four components:

- A statement of the acceptance

- A statement of what is to be done

- A statement of how thoroughly the job is to be done (called the "conditions of satisfaction")

- The time frame

Here are some additional guidelines that help such mini-contracts to succeed:

- Play fair. Your word is your bond: don't agree to a task unless you actually believe you can do it.

- If you suspect you can't complete the task the way it was requested, speak up before you agree to it.

- You must discuss changes in any aspect of the agreement BEFORE the agreement is accepted or as soon as the needed modification becomes apparent. You can't wait until 10 minutes before the deadline and ask for an extension. Not fair.

- Failure to keep an agreement will carry consequences.

Here is an actual example. My partner asked me to wash her car. Specifically, she asked me to wash her car's exterior and vacuum the interior within two hours. Everything that was on the car seats was to be brought into the house and placed on a kitchen counter.

Here's what the agreement looked like.

- I agree to wash, rinse, and dry the exterior of your car so no water spots remain.

- I further agree to bring into the house and place on the kitchen counter everything that is inside the car that is not built in.

- After removing items from the car, I will vacuum the car's interior.

- I agree to do all this within the next two hours.

- If I fail, you get to pick where we go to dinner.

Not too tough. The benefit of speaking the agreement is that it ensures that you and your partner understand and agree on everything that is important with the task. It removes doubt and fosters connection.

Larger (longer-term) difficult tasks involve different questions depending upon the type of difficulty you're encountering. For example, if you're taking on a challenge such as "working on your personal relationship" you'll need to outline a plan of attack able to sustain you for years. By the way, you can't treat all difficult tasks the same way. Some demanding tasks require acceptance while others require aggression; some require responsiveness while others require stoicism. Knowing the kind of difficulty you are facing makes a lot of difference.

Anyway, here are a few words on various approaches/solutions to difficult tasks:

- If the difficulty involves one-time luck, then you're either in luck or not in luck. Win/lose.

- If the difficulty is not a one-time affair, then you have to decide how much work it will take to accomplish the task without luck already on your side.

- If the difficulty involves both luck and skill and is to be a repeated experience (such as playing the stock market with a "system"), you must put yourself in a position to be lucky. Using the stock or commodities markets as examples, "putting yourself in a position to be lucky" involves such things as *loss tolerance, risk management,* and *patience.* If the system actually works, you have to be able to steel yourself against consecutive losing strings because those will only be noise. Regardless of the endeavor, you will have to account for the possibility your luck may end tomorrow, or it might not. You have to be prepared to be adaptable; you have to be prepared to tolerate ambiguity. (I used to run a commodity futures trading company, in case you wondered about this paragraph.)

- If the difficulty concerns in-depth mastery of a skill or a field of study, then buckle down and get aggressive. Find someone who has been successful in this field and model yourself after them: find a coach. Rewards tend to correlate to the number of study hours you put in.

- If the difficulty involves mastering a wide breadth of information to perform a task at a certain level of proficiency, be patient and focus on small gains. Celebrate little improvements. Embrace boredom and build habits that stay the same for years.

It's hard…

It's hard to look inside yourself and see how you were built.

It's hard to change what you have become.

This chapter explores my favorite collection of personal variables. In my experience, the more you understand how you work, the easier it will be for you to choose what to work on and what to ignore.

I'd like to start you out with some quotes from people who have captured aspects of this process in particularly concise phrases.

- You will never find time for anything. If you want time you must make it. (Charles Robert Buxton)

- Success is the ability to go from failure to failure without losing your enthusiasm. (Winston Churchill)

- Opportunities are usually disguised as hard work, so most people don't recognize them. (Ann Landers)

- The "problem" is lack of direction, not lack of time. We all have twenty-four hour days. (Zig Ziglar)

- Don't wish it were easier, wish you were better. (Jim Roh)

- The questions you ask are more important than the things you could ever say. (Tom Freese)

- Excellence is not a skill. It's an attitude. (Ralph Marston)

Chapter Two
Perspectives and Personality

You are a very complicated person. So is your partner. So is your neighbor. So am I. Our backgrounds have made us who we are. Our current behaviors have been shaped by our (unique) interpretation of our experiences. That is, from infancy, something happened, it had an impact on us, we judged that impact to be good or bad and we learned a mini-lesson that slightly modified our reaction to that person, place, or thing. Over time, our collection of reactions to our interpretation of events has created our current personalities.

I like writing. I get to pull together information and experiences of a lifetime and apply them to a single topic. In this case, the topic is communication theory and practice.

This is one of my favorite chapters because I get to share some techniques that have helped improve my own communication skills. Much of this chapter stems from the world of Neuro-Lingusitic Programming (NLP). I hope you find it useful.

I've divided this chapter into two sections:

- Perspectives on life
- Personality variables

I once heard a satirical joke about how few good ideas people had. They said that if the average person has 10,000 ideas per day, that the same average person had 99.999% of those same ideas the day before, and the day before, and the day before. Actually, the hidden problem concerned overworked ideas.

Let's see if we can come up with some fresh ideas. But we'll have to work together on this. I can only pose the questions and areas for you to explore: you have to do the work.

Communication success is a product of who you are and how you've come to speak as you currently do. To change the way you speak, it might help to understand how you came to speak this way. That may take some soul-searching.

Do you speak rather like your mother or father? Can you recall any guidance they gave you on the topic of communications? Did your family stress education and the importance of having a large vocabulary? Do you enjoy reading books (or taking classes) to help you understand how to make it easier for others to understand YOU? Most people who read that paragraph would say: "What?" So, let's delve into this a bit.

Perspectives on Life

I've compiled brief descriptions of some of the ways people differ as adults based on their own characteristics and upbringing. You'll have to expand this list as you run across topics that are more relevant to your own relationships. I'm just trying to get you thinking along these lines:

- Perspectives and upbringing

- Giving/receiving gifts

- Rewards

- The meaning of time

- Points of view

- Mental processing speed combined with differences in work experiences

- Thinking styles and working styles

- Reactance vs. resistance

Background (Perspectives) and Upbringing

What you know and what you think you know governs your view of your world and your responses to it. However, as Gerald Nierenberg pointed out in his book *How to Give and Receive Advice,* "Your facts are built on the sands of your assumptions." Succinctly, that means that you don't know what you don't know, and when you express an opinion based on what you *think* you know, your belief about that subject is expressed as an unfounded assumption or assertion.

(Note: If you want a fresh and surprisingly profound look at how cultural differences have long-term impact on individual behavior, I'd urge you to read Malcolm Gladwell's book: *Outliers.*)

Let's look at how people view relationships. Some believe that Fate determines whether or not relationships work out. They believe that relationships are natural-occurring pairings that either do or do not succeed. Others believe that relationships require constant attention and tending to ensure that each person's needs and wants are honored. The fact that you're reading this book suggests that you're part of this second group.

In my experience, successful long-term relationships require a lot of work by both parties. The more work you put into the relationship, the smoother it runs. When problems arise, it's often due to one person's assumptions regarding the meaning of what the other person said or did that turned out not to be exactly correct.

To the extent that those involved come from similar backgrounds—social class, status, education, business experience, and travel, to name a few areas—responses to the "somethings" that happen in life will be similar. To the extent that your backgrounds are dissimilar, you're likely to experience some areas of misunderstanding and friction. I hasten to add that background differences don't make one or the other of you more worthy/valuable/right—just different.

If you find yourself in a situation in which one of you cares more than the other on how something is done (or how to behave in certain situations), you might want to recall the lessons of your childhood. I suspect you'll find some parental echoes still ringing in your head.

Oh, and these echoes are not benign. These echoes have guided your behavior and have strongly influenced your choice of who you have befriended and who you've avoided. In fact, I suspect you'll find that these echoes of from your childhood have formed your assumptions about who is or is not a suitable partner. Just to check that out, you might ask yourself AND your partner to rate on a 1-10 scale (where 10 means: "I completely agree") how much you agree with statements such as these.

- Sloppy body, sloppy mind.

- Television dumbs-down society.

- Your word is your bond: it is the basis of your character. Dishonesty is a character flaw.

- Driving over the speed limit violates your agreement to be a law-abiding citizen.

- It's better to be interested than interesting.

- Both partners in a relationship should be transparent to the other: no secrets.

- The way you keep your house reflects the way you think and what you value.

- All people have worth.

- It's more important to be nice than to be smart.

- Most wealthy people were simply lucky.

To the extent that you and your partner have substantially different views on ideas such as these (and you can certainly make up your own list), there will be an ideological mismatch between the two of you. I can't say how that mismatch will express itself, but it will. The next time you have an upset with your partner, you might want to tease out the different beliefs you each hold about the "something" that happened. You can't hold your partner responsible for their part of the upset if they were following their beliefs about the issues of the upset. When it comes to two people fitting into a relationship, it helps to figure out what you don't know in order to be able to consider changing those core beliefs in order to be a better partner.

This is a good place to stick in an important observation concerning *expectations*.

Think back to when you were in school. If you did all the required work, did that earn you that an "A" or a "C?" Personally, completing all the work correctly only meant that I was now at the stage where I could work a little harder (beyond the basic knowledge) to achieve a "B," or work a lot harder to earn an "A" for exceptional effort. This plays out in daily life: Are you expecting an "A" partner or a "C" partner. If your expectations are different, one of you may find that what they hoped would be a "gift of service" is really a personal sacrifice. It's hard to recover from disillusionment.

By the way, if you're having frequent upsets over a fairly wide range of issues, you may want to take a broader view of who the two of you are and reassess why in the world you wish to be a couple.

Positional awareness: Some people are brought up to respect their elders; others are brought up that old people are simply old, slow, and living in the past. Some people are brought up to respect authority; others constantly test the authority of those who cannot affect their future (who do not have "fate control" over them). Some people are brought up to offer respect freely; others require respect to be earned. Some people are brought up to value everyone; others are taught only to value people who are clearly productive.

As my father would say: "It takes all kinds to make a horse race."

So: how does this relate to your own personal communications?

Importantly, your underlying views about class, status, education, and role affect how you interact with everyone in your life. For example, if you are a schoolteacher, you are in the dominant position with respect to your students and in the subordinate position with the school's administrators. Similarly, the police officer who pulls you over for a speeding ticket is dominant to you but subordinate to those to whom they report. Even the police chief, who is in the dominant to all their officers, is subordinate to the mayor. And so it goes. At the very top, leaders are subordinate to public opinion.

The message, though, is that the way you were raised to react to authority figures will influence not only how you have "discussions" with your partner, but also how you communicate with everyone in your world. Those who have been brought up to be very discrete and respectful around those they perceive have more power, authority, or influence will speak with more caution and reflection than those who have been brought up that authority is taken, not granted.

This little section isn't meant to give you communication strategies based on your own sensitivity to someone's "position" in your world. It is only designed to raise the question so you can consider it when you are reviewing your next conversation that hit some rough patches.

Needs vs. wants. I need food, I want sex. Oh, err. That probably should have read: I need food, I want cake. Politically correct and all that. One of you could be thinking: "I want to read, I need to clean the house," while the other might be thinking: "I want to read, I need to do something affirming for my partner."

That brings up the obvious question, what is it that you really need? You probably can't get everything you **want**, so it may be worthwhile to identify what you believe you really **need**.

In the world of research from which I come, there's a prophetic saying about obtaining research data:

> What you have is not what you want,
> What you want is not what you need, and
> What you need costs too much.

Obviously, there are costs involved in all relationships. There are emotional costs, intellectual costs, opportunity costs, and so on. In a relationship, if you combine the costs of your *wants* and *needs*, you may develop a project cost-overrun. Personal budget cost-overruns usually lead to debt buildup on emotional or financial credit cards. Not good.

This budget-busting condition develops when you have a lot of *wants* from your partner but not a lot of discernment about what you actually *need* from them. Without that discernment, there's the risk of getting upset over something that you *want* but don't actually *need*. Here are some quotes that speak more to *wants* than to *needs*, but I find them very insightful.

- "The indisputable first step to getting the things you want out of life is this: Decide what you want." [Source unknown]

- "One half of knowing what you want is knowing what you must give up before you get it." [Sidney Howard]

- "If you don't get what you want, it is a sign either that you did not seriously want it, or that you tried to bargain over the price." [Rudyard Kipling, 1865-1936]

- "If you don't have what you want, you are not committed to it 100%." [Source unknown]

- "There are two things to aim at in life: first, to get what you want; and after that to enjoy it. Only the wisest of people achieve the second." [Logan Pearsall Smith, 1865-1946]

Separating needs from wants—and determining what you need out of a relationship—influences how you will react to one another. Once you can discuss each of your needs, you have the opportunity to build a workable future. Your solutions may not live up to your fantasies, but they will be the best solutions with respect to the longevity of your relationship.

Inclusive vs. Exclusive

Do you tend to like everybody or do you tend to have "judgments and considerations" about some kinds of people? Are you comfortable speaking with a homeless person? With a grocery clerk? With a physicist? With an elected politician? How about speaking with someone dressed poorly and then someone who appears to have just come from a photo shoot for a fashion magazine? Do your friends tend to be quite different from one another or pretty much the same?

This issue of inclusion/exclusion affects your communication ability. One's ability to speak comfortably is linked to whether or not you even wish to spend time speaking with someone. THAT assessment is often driven by your pre-judgments about whether or not you want to have anything to do with the person in the first place.

Here some polarizing sayings I've picked up over the years that demonstrate the "inclusive/exclusive" issue. Although I include citations for such quotations when they are available, I have none recorded for these three:

- There are two kinds of people: those who want to get things done and those who want to be right.

- In a rather general way, people can be classed into three groups:

  ○ Those who make things happen,
  ○ Those who watch things happen, and
  ○ Those who wonder what just happened.

- There are two types of people: those who separate people into groups and those who do not.

My friend Karen Martin (an author in her own right) has a slightly different way of describing people who accept others and those who do not. She refers to *polka-dot* and *plaid* people. Polka-dot people see differences between themselves and others and will isolate or exclude many/most people from being candidates for friendship. She observes that in many cases, polka-dot people socialize based upon those perceived differences and have judgments about a person's physical size/weight, how the person thinks or expresses themselves, whether the person is part of a particular group/sub-culture, how smart/lucid/articulate another person is, and so on. They may let instant class/status/education distinctions color their willingness to develop friendships outside their comfort zones.

She goes on: "Actually, I believe they decide they are inside the polka-dot with all of the other people who think and act as they do. It can be just as inclusive as it is exclusive. Polka-dot people are very loyal to others in the circle. In contrast to polka-dot people, plaid people, find value/worth in everyone and appreciate people for their individuality and the different perspectives they bring to bear on life. They may actually accept an individual based on an interest or a view that is not congruent with any of their other values." (Private discussion.)

This polka-dot vs. plaid distinction is closely related to how people view the scarcity or abundance of *love*. Some people view love as *conditional*, while others view it as *unconditional*. That is, those who put conditions on their love for another would say: "I'll love you so long as you do/learn or grow/behave in this way." Those who practice *unconditional* love would say: "I love you, I'm not going anywhere, nothing you can do or say will ever alter my love for you; now—let's talk about what you just did."

There is another distinction to be made about the scarcity or abundance of love that affects relationships. Some people see *love* as a scarce commodity, and if their partner begins to make an emotional connection with another person, they may feel as though he/she has lost the amount of his love that their partner is now giving to the new person. Abandonment alarms go off in their head. Therein lies jealousy, stress, conflict, and emotional trauma. In some cases, the partner who wishes to connect emotionally (not necessarily sexually, by the way) may develop anger towards their partner for such conditional love ("I'll love you so long as you only love me."). As you can imagine, such situations cause some degree of emotional separation (for self-protection) and adds a layer of stress to their communication.

Now, on the other side of the spectrum, many people see love as infinitely abundant. For them, their partner is welcome to have multiple emotionally-close friends of either gender. These people adopt the attitude that encouraging their partner to have multiple close emotional connections helps to keep their primary relationship fresh and focused. These people know why they are a couple and bring new ideas and experiences back to one another, further stabilizing their union.

This distinction between viewing love as scarce or abundant is a key factor when it comes to polyamorous vs. monogamous households.

Giving/Receiving Gifts

This may seem an odd item to place in a chapter dealing with assumptions, but I've found it to be very important. Gifts are a form of communication, they are a form of acknowledgment, a way of saying, "I really like you and I'm thinking about you." It's a tangible symbol.

For many people, gifts are an "I love you" statement. These people derive joy and pleasure from shopping for the gift, wrapping it, and finding that special card to include with it. Similarly, if they don't receive gifts for special occasions or as special rewards, they feel devalued; their feelings get hurt.

In a relationship in which only one person uses gifts as a love message, a problem can arise. If the non-gift-oriented person misses the love message, they may not react as the gift-giver had intended.

In extreme cases, the gift may trigger a number of negative thoughts in the head of the person who is non-gift oriented:

- "I didn't get a gift for him/her."

- "My gift isn't as well thought-out as the gift I'm receiving."

- "Where in the world am I going to put THAT?"

- "Oh, geez—we said we weren't going to exchange gifts and I didn't get him/her anything."

- "Money, money, ah, the expense!"

People who don't communicate love by giving gifts may view a gift as another piece of stuff they have to discard or give away. These people often look at gift-giving as an obligation of the Holidays, rather than an "I like/love you" statement. By the way, let me hasten to add that those who interpret gifts as messages of love do not necessarily require the gift to be expensive. A little *I love you* chocolate on the pillow at night can be a huge emotional boost for such people.

There's more to giving and receiving a gift than the act itself. In relationships, it helps to know the other person's language of love.

Reactance vs. Resistance

Sooner or later, you are going to encounter *resistance* and/ or *reactance* when speaking with someone. The difference between these words is important.

Reactance is generally a minor thing, but noticeable. You say something the other person hadn't expected and they react. Their eyes widen; they stiffen. You might trigger their reaction to say "no" to an idea put to them without building up to it. With knowledge and practice, you can learn to speak in ways that don't trigger reactance in others and ways of calming a person's reactance. (See, for example: *Crucial Conversations* by Kerry Patterson and Joseph Grenny, 2010)

Reactance is usually a temporary flaring related to hurt feelings. You say something and your hearer gives you a look of defiance, a little expression of exasperation or disgust, a rolling of eyes, or a direct challenge that questions what you just said. This is particularly common when a new couple is still working out the power structure. There is still testing to determine who is leading and who is following and the authority and responsibility of each person.

Reactance unaddressed can transition to *resistance.*

Resistance can be unconscious: it can build up over time as a result of prior conversations/experiences with this person. This is troubling. This is likely to be a substantial signal that something fundamental is amiss between the two of you; this requires some careful probing and questioning. Whether in a work or personal setting, it's been my experience that resistance signals one person's failure to hear/see/feel the other person's signals for help/relief in some area. Again, my continual theme: communication is improved when you have good listening skills and can appreciate the world through your partner's eyes.

When you encounter resistance, you are likely to want to reestablish stability in order to work through the situation. In such cases, I recommend you consider changing the mood. More formally, this is called a *state change*. "State" means "emotional state." State change is most important if you've suddenly lost rapport with the other person. Perhaps one of you said or did something not taken well by the other person. You can ignore it and continue as though nothing happened (one or both of you are now "stuffing" your emotional reactions), or you can try to fix it. To fix this "it," you'll want to know something about how to use state change to get back to rapport.

As this is not a book on learning state change and other Neuro-Linguistic Programming (NLP) techniques, I'll give only one example.

Perhaps the easiest way of changing your emotional state is to alter your physical position. If sitting, stand up. If standing, sit down or walk around. There is a caution, here. If the person with whom you're speaking is emotionally upset or angry, changing your physical position may be interpreted as a threat and escalate the situation. The more you know about yourself and your reactions under stress (and the more you know about your hearer), the better you'll be at managing such an exchange. At the very least, breathe slowly and deeply and keep control of your facial muscles.

Rewards

In the same way that people have different views about giving and receiving gifts, people vary in their need to receive acknowledgement for their service. If you do a job well, do you expect to be recognized for it, or do you assume that your role in life is to do jobs well as part of who you are? This transfers to your life in a relationship.

I suspect that there are two categories of cultural conditioning that influence the different viewpoints. In a general sense, some are brought up to identify tasks and to complete them competently. Thus (in the most general way), the idea of *completing a task correctly* becomes the norm; they don't expect to be congratulated about it. If told to keep the house in a certain way on a daily basis, this type of person probably doesn't expect their partner nightly to say: "Oh, honey, you've done a good job keeping the house neat and clean." It's in the job description; of course it's performed perfectly.

However, (in the most general way) those socialized as nurturers are more likely to want their work to be recognized. Frequently. The longer they go without hearing words of recognition for their good work, the more they will exhibit resistance/upset traits. Left unattended, the next stage may lead to an emotional outburst about how little they feel appreciated. Left unattended beyond that point, you'll start to see emotional withdrawal. This is often expressed as withdrawal from sex (not helped if their partner is sexually self-centered, but that's the topic for a different book).

Personally, when it concerned normal and routine duties, I found it hard to learn to provide daily and ongoing performance recognition for one of my former partners. I am *extremely* inner-directed and if someone congratulates me for doing something I see as routine, my knee-jerk reaction is that the person wants something from me. It takes me a minute to figure out what is being said and to realize that this is a gratuitous compliment without some ulterior motive. It's actually jarring to me when someone compliments me in any area. However, I have Asperger Syndrome, and that may account for my reaction.

As with most topics involving assumptions, this is an area you'll need to work through on your own. Not only must you figure out what your partner needs by way of affirmation, but also the range of statements/acts that will even be **recognized** as an affirmation. That is, while flowers may work with one person, candies may be better for another, while a simple "good job" works for a third. This speaks to your language of love. How do you say *I love you* in a way that your partner gets it? I'm told that in some relationships, the husband turning his paycheck over to his spouse is about all the "I love you" she's likely to get—or perhaps want.

The Meaning of Time

Time is to humans as water is to fish—you don't think about it, but your life's journey depends upon it. Let me begin this section with a quote from *Time for Life: The surprising ways Americans use their time.* John Robinson, Geoffrey Goodbey, and Robert Putnam.

"Many people have developed dysfunctional attitudes toward time as an infinitely expandable resource... As numerous scholars have observed, two modes of human consciousness exist. One perceives reality as separate objects existing in three-dimensional space and linear time. The other, which may be called spiritual, holistic, or transpersonal, views reality as a series of relationships among all things that is part of some universal consciousness.

"People who subscribe to the first mode typically lead ego-centered, competitive, goal-oriented lives... Such a consciousness is related to how time is viewed and the extent to which pace-of-life is an issue. Those who cannot derive satisfaction from ordinary activities of everyday life will always be rushed to construct another basis of satisfaction."

I've had this same conceptual conflict with a long-term partner. I'd say: "Meet me at 3:00" and she seemed to hear: "Meet me about 3:00" and then not understand why I was upset that she arrived at 3:10. Her sense of the importance of time was simply *different* than mine.

Clashes would occur when she was running errands (or returning from work) and forgot to let me know she'd been delayed. She would come in beaming with love and contentment to be greeted by an upset partner. Many times, I'd been fuming that she wasn't home when she said she would be, and hadn't called to alert me. I had "Things Planned" and now those "Things" weren't going to get done because she was Late. My reactions (out of proportion to the event) stunned and hurt her. With good reason, I say in hindsight. Unfortunately, my reactions often affected the remainder of our day/evening.

It took us some time to realize that we viewed time differently. Once we could name it, we could fix it and we designed ways to avoid that particular conflict. For the sake of illustration, here was our work-around:

- If I had particular time-sensitive need for her after work or after errands, I communicate those to her ahead of time.

- If she had to work past 5:30, she was to call me as soon as she realized that, and either provide a better time estimate or tell me she didn't yet know when she could leave. In this second case, she was also to call me when she was in her car, heading home. (I worked from home and liked my work day to end with her arrival home.)

- If she was running errands and it became apparent that she'd be home later than we'd discussed, she would call me to let me know about the change in plans.

(Note: re-reading this, I come off as overbearingly controlling. That's not it. I worked from home and needed to know roughly when I should close down for the day. That process took about 30 minutes. I would start to prepare for her arrival as soon as I knew she had left work. That way, I was in the right "headspace" when she got home.)

Joel Bennett, author of the extremely meaty and profound book *Time and Intimacy: A New Science of Personal Relationships,* lists eight basic functions of time as they can support or tear down a relationship. As these eight points are really communication issues, I've listed them here in a shortened and edited version:

1   **Disruption**: When it comes to communication and relationships, focus and concentration are your friends: disruptions affect the quality of your bonding.

2   **Scheduling**: Realize that your individual and joint decisions to budget or allocate time to specific tasks, activities, or recreations are a form of *time shaping*. The two of you are working together to determine what you are going to do within a certain time frame. This is good for relationship bonding.

3   **Timing**: Since change is all around us, it helps your relationship when you both can be flexible about what it takes to make you feel happy and emotionally close. This includes a sense of the right time to do certain things

as well as knowing when to work separately or together to accomplish some task.

4   **Rhythmic Synchronicity**: This has to do with understanding the way your various rhythms—biological, hormonal, and sleep-wake cycles—are in or out of sync with your partner. Taken more broadly, it affects your general success with communication, as synchronicity influences many aspects of life.

5   **Pacing**: The degree to which one considers and regulates the length of time, interval, series, or sequence of actions they take when approaching or avoiding a particular task.

6   **Routines**: The ways in which your work or personal relationship structure dictates your social habits. (If you have some kinds of jobs, there are places you can't be seen: if one of you has a strong dislike for some place, out of courtesy for your partner, you don't go there.)

7   **Transition**: Ways in which conditions change the structure or form of the relationship. This can include changes in roles, changes in levels of cooperation, or in degrees of obedience.

8   **Time Transcendence**: The ways in which both nurturing and chaotic conditions enable us to move past our limited viewpoints about linear time. This includes events that provide feelings of joy, ecstasy, wonder, mystery, or a sense of timelessness due to absorption or immersion in the relationship. (Is he trying to describe an *ecstatic state*?)

Time is actually a concept worth researching and discussing in some depth. Until I read Bennett's book I had no idea of the many ways that *time* affects communication in general— and specifically affects the inner workings of relationships. I strongly recommend the book to you.

Personality Variables

Many things contribute to who we are. Some of us know more about ourselves than others; some of us actively search out little windows through which to view ourselves. I'm one of those, and over the years, I've collected a number of ways about thinking of others and myself. Here, I'm only briefly listing them. If you like them, you now have some ideas about areas to research.

Note: To explore this material in greater depth, you might consider: *Unlimited Power: The New Science Of Personal Achievement* by Anthony Robbins, 1997. Also, you'll learn this material if you decide to learn more about Neuro-Linguistic Programming. These thinking loops are called "meta-programs" and a simple Internet search will give you lots of additional information.

None of these meta-programs are particularly important in isolation; together they paint a particular kind of picture of you and the person with whom you're speaking. These all must be discovered through probing conversation, which is why they're in this book:

- Toward or away from;
- External vs. internal frame of reference;

- Sorting by self or sorting by others;
- Matcher or mismatcher;
- Possibility vs. necessity;
- Independent vs. Cooperative Working Styles;
- Process vs. Product Thinking.

Toward or Away From

Some people choose a path because they are moving *towards* some goal. They are attracted towards something. Such people become involved with their partner because they believe that together, they can achieve some goal that would otherwise be unattainable. This is commonly referred to as synergy.

Other people choose a path in order to *avoid* something. They want to stay away from something they fear (abandonment, isolation, living singly). This is why people enter relationships they really know aren't great: they want to avoid living alone, to avoid financial problems, etc.

Here's an example:

- Some people make investments because they are motivated to move *towards* financial gain while other people do *not* make investments because they are motivated to move *away from* the risk of losing money. (I used to be both a stock and commodities broker.)

- In the workplace, careers can be seen to be extensions of *toward* or *away from* viewpoints. Salesmen are *towards* people because they can get people excited about possibilities. CPAs and most lawyers are *away from* people. They spend their careers keeping clients out of trouble.

As you think about conversations at work and at home, consider whether you and your hearer are aligned in the ways you approach (or avoid) life and life experiences. The closer the two of you operate in this dynamic, the more you can support one another. I'm a "towards" person, but I lived closely with an "away from" person for many years. It was a challenge working with her, as most things other than staying at home involved some *risk*. *Risk* of not liking the party, city, restaurant, or movie; risk of having to speak with someone. To her, risk meant, "threat"; threat meant, "Don't do it." We stayed home a lot.

Differences in approaches to life can/will play out in conversations. If you listen closely, you may find that preferences and decisions are based on the "towards vs. away-from" dynamic. That clue can help you develop conversation profiles for that person.

External or Internal Frame of Reference

This is a brief discussion about how people are motivated. The concept of personal motivation is often divided between those who are *internally motivated* and those who are *externally motivated*.

Those who are **internally motivated** look at what they accomplish and are either satisfied or dissatisfied with the result. They don't need anyone else to approve of their accomplishment or to acknowledge them for having done it. They work well in isolation.

By comparison, those who are **externally motivated** often feel accomplishment or success once someone has recognized that accomplishment (won an award, met a quota), or they have succeeded in meeting a team goal.

Note: While motivations may differ, goals may be the same. Some people think that one frame of reference is better than another, but that's the same fallacy as thinking that being a boss is "better" than being a worker. While neither is true, there is a catch: When it comes to thinking of oneself as internally or externally motivated, your self-assessment suffers from what is called "participant-observer bias." Someone else will have to help you to understand your own frame of reference. You're too close to yourself.

Just to confuse the issue, the degree to which you are internally or externally motivated is situational. The most internally motivated person in the world can easily become externally motivated. Think about being in the military and having to follow orders. Your success in advancing in rank depends upon what *others* think of you and your performance NOT what you think of yourself and your own performance. So, these terms are amorphous. For our purposes, today, we are looking at *frame of reference* only as it relates to your communication skills.

These motivation concepts concern how people react to completing a job or task—as well as how they initiate the next job or task. For example, while an externally motivated person may only work at their job for the paycheck, an internally motivated person might do the same task or job for free because it gives them satisfaction or fulfillment.

- At one extreme, you can imagine internally motivated people persisting at a task they like even though others tell them they aren't very good at it. They don't care what others think.

- At the other extreme, you can imagine externally motivated people working very hard at something they don't much like in order to win a trophy, make more money, buy a bigger boat (etc.) in order to feel that others see them as "successful."

There can be HUGE differences between how you and your partner feel affirmed in your work and personal lives. Here are some examples:

- Using an external frame of reference, one person may stop doing something that is not continually reinforced. This is not likely to be well received by someone who uses an internal frame of reference. The person with the internal reference frame may come to view the other person as a bad match. This isn't good at work or at home.

- Using an internal frame of reference (not seeking any outside reinforcement whatsoever), the person may chafe at outside comments about the way they do a job. This builds relationship friction and is not likely to be good for a work or personal relationship.

Using opposing frames of reference without realizing it (and talking about it) may make it hard to understand the other person's actions and reactions.

Sorting-by-Self or Sorting by Others

In the area of communication theory, the NLP concept of *sorting-by-self* or *sorting-by-others* is extremely important. It often sits at the core of misunderstandings, hurt feelings, and upsets. In situations where one is called on to make a decision that could affect others, those who think of themselves first give answers that reflect that thinking pattern and vice versa. Those who sort by others first consider the impact their statement would have on those others.

Here is how this can play out at home.

This person sorts primarily by self. While out running some errands, they remember they need something that would take additional time not previously discussed with their domestic partner. They insert this errand among the others because it would save **them** time in the long run. However, they are now getting home an hour later than discussed. Because they sort by self, it does not occur to them to call home to let their Significant Other know of the changed plans.

Scene shift: The errand-running partner gets home an hour late...

If the at-home partner *also* sorts by self, they may be upset because they had expected their mate home an hour ago. If this situation has happened before, this partner may become angry at not having been called/notified of the changed arrival time. In extreme cases (of which I have ample personal experience), this person may view this situation as a violation of trust: their partner didn't keep their word about when they'd be home.

One person is angry they were not considered; the other person is remorseful that their actions caused this anger—they were simply late. One person is questioning the other's integrity (keeping one's word); the other person is questioning their partner's values and love.

This is seriously not good. This is a relationship-threatening situation.

Alternative behavior: The errand-running partner could learn to keep their at-home partner informed about changes in errands and arrival time. The at-home partner could learn to defuse those situations by asking emotionally-neutral questions dealing with *intent* before choosing to become reactive and emotional. For example, the at-home partner could ask simply: "Hi, Honey! I've been worried. What delayed you?"

Once they understand *why* their partner was an hour late, they can work together to develop strategies to avoid similar future conflicts. (Of course, the next alternative is to say: "Oh, I get it now! Thanks.")

Said another way - If the first person was a *sorts-by-others* type, they would have called their partner to inform them of the change in arrival time. If the second person was a *sorts-by-others* type, they would have recognized that additional errands were run causing an ease in their partner or relationship.

However, sorting by others is not always a preferred method. My current partner sacrifices her own needs as she sorts by others. A more extreme situation than mentioned above. She will know her needs, and yet give up those needs in order to facilitate the needs of another. Not a good match when her partner is a sorts by others person too. This is the "What do you want for dinner tonight", "I don't care, what do you want?", "I don't care, whatever you want" issue.

Understanding and communication will help these personality types have successful relationships.

Process vs. Product Orientation

Conflicts over *how* a job gets done can be confused with the "sorts-by-self / sorts-by-others" paradigm we just covered. In the prior case, it doesn't occur to the "sorts-by-self" person that anyone else really cares **what** they do, while the "sorts-by-others" person cares how others would interpret their actions.

When it comes to completing a task, some people care primarily **how** the job gets done, others care primarily **that** the job gets done. For example, in a work setting, process managers will say: "You are to be at work for eight hours starting at 8am." They may care that your body is there more than they care about your output. At the other end of the spectrum, product managers will say: "You are to get your job done and I don't care whether you are physically in the office as you're completing tasks on schedule."

In a home setting, one or the other of you may want certain tasks completed in a particular way. For example, when we moved in together, Jen told me to alphabetize spices in the spice rack and to organize the pantry in a certain way. Okay. I got that. This is a simple example of *process-driven* leadership. How the job is done matters to the person asking you to do it.

This process/product dichotomy can lead to conflict. The product-oriented person just wants to get the job done. The process-oriented person wants that same job done in a certain way and objects when that way is not followed. This situation arises when the person being asked to do something is thinking: "Okay, I agree this needs to get done, but I think I know how to do it better (faster, cheaper) than you do."

Here is an example with Person A and Person B:

- "Person A" asks "Person B" to do X project in Y fashion.

- "Person B" uses the Y approach only once or twice before deciding it is nutty (or unimportant or harder).

- "Person B" changes the way they are dong X project from the Y approach to their own Z approach.

- After some time, "Person A" realizes that "Person B" is not doing X in Y fashion, and comments about it.

- "Person B" becomes bristly. They don't see any reason why X should be done in Y fashion, especially since they've now successfully completed it using their preferred Z approach.

Mismatches concerning how tasks are done—regardless of how they ultimately turn out—create stress. If conflicts are frequent, one or the other person may conclude that differences in working and thinking styles suggests:

- They are not good long-term relationship candidates,
- That compromise is unattainable, or
- That sacrifice by one or the other parties is inevitable.

If neither party cares how projects are completed (or they have elected to give up control so long as they *are* completed), then there is no relationship threat at all.

Bottom line: people are different; their reactions are different. In work and in personal relationships, people choose the degree of control they wish to exercise. The degree of control they *wish* to exercise and the degree of control they actually *can* exercise are often different. Relationship friction builds up when one person inhibits the other person's expression of control. This is another significant area that can improve or degrade a relationship.

Matcher vs. Mismatcher

Are you hunting for common ground when you start speaking with someone new? Are you listening for things the person says that resonate with you? Are you trying to establish rapport? When you're thinking about your partner, are you thinking of the many ways you're similar? If yes, you are what's called a "matcher" when it concerns initial reactions to someone. (We brushed by this concept previously in the section inclusion vs. exclusion. You may recall the discussion about *polka-dot* vs. *plaid* people. This takes the concept a bit further.)

The opposite, of course, is a "mismatcher." This describes someone who immediately starts cataloging the ways this person is different from them. Differences such as regional dialect, word choice, dress, posture, lucidity, clarity, and vocabulary, to name a few, stand up and waive. Mismatchers typically ask themselves whether they even want to establish rapport with this person.

At a subtler level, some people use two or more refining methods of sorting others. They may use one form for initial sorting, then the other form to note exceptions. That is, some matchers look for common elements in a person or situation, but also note mismatches that are exceptions to the sameness.

"You're killing me," you're saying? "Hogwash and gobbledygook!" you're saying. OK, try this.

Let's start when you meet someone. You're basically a mis-matcher. All the differences between you and this person pop up in your head. But, as you're speaking, you start to find common ground. You seem to like similar activities. You enjoyed attending the same conference. You both also appreciate X or Y or Z. Maybe you can maintain a conversation.

That's called a "mismatcher with exceptions to sameness." Its cousin is a "matcher with additions for sameness." As most people do some of each, most of us fall within one of these two groups.

Examples:

- A "matcher with additions for sameness" would be likely to thrive in positions involving social interaction. This person will initially identify with everyone they meet and seem relaxed and friendly. As their conversation moves on, this person may notice a few things that are not like him/herself, but they are not big deals.

- A "mismatcher with exceptions for sameness" would be less comfortable in social settings and may belong to a club or social group of like-minded folk. While their immediate reaction is stand-offish, they'll usually warm up if you can engage them in conversation.

The matcher/mismatcher parable is usually expressed as having a "half-empty glass" vs. "half-full glass" viewpoint. Friction can arise when you are partnered with someone with polar ways of viewing events and people unless understanding of the different sorting styles are discussed. A matcher, in a social situation, is going to be much more comfortable than the mis-matcher. They can use each other's strengths to support the other within the relationship.

Possibility vs. Necessity

Okay, this is somewhat close to the "toward or away from" discussion a few pages back. This has a slight twist.

Some people start/do a task because they are looking for pos-sibilities that might open for them. It's something they want, not something they feel they *have* to do. They are *pulled,* not *pushed* into action. They are at the cause of their actions, not at the effect of limiting debts and obligations. They are less motivated by what they *have* to do than by what they *want* to do. These people are always searching for options, choices, experiences, etc. Often, it's a gift when they do something for another.

On the opposing side, others are most motivated by *necessity.* They do a thing because (for some reason) they feel they are obliged to do it. They aren't pulled to act because of a new possibility, they feel forced to take what the world has laid be-fore them. When they need a new job, new house, new partner, they take what comes around and what seems available. Fate controls their options and opportunities. Often, when they do something for another, it's a sacrifice. In a relationship, such a person may say they "live in quiet desperation," feeling they have no control over their future.

Relationship stress can build up if one person operates from possibility and the other operates from necessity. As an ex-ample, if the person operating from possibility proposes a new project to the person operating from necessity, they (the possibility person) may be met with a reaction that falls somewhere between massively disinterested to uncooperative. The "necessity" person sees no *need* for the new skill. Obviously, this can be very frustrating for both people. Frustration equals stress equals unstable relationship.

Here's an example. Two people have become a couple in midlife. One person is a good photographer; the other person is creative but isn't interested in photography. The photographer knows their new partner could help in a number of ways. The disinterested partner sees no need to learn any of the skills that would help the photographer-partner. Disharmony results.

Some people are pulled towards possibility as part of who they are; others are generally satisfied with whatever life sends their way.

Independent vs. Cooperative
Would you rather be right or would you rather be happy? You can choose which fights to fight.

Communication isn't that tough. You have the power to make communication easier for yourself. This is a book both of generalities and of specifics. In a general way, you have to give up the attitude that *you're right* in order to "hear" what the other person is saying. Arguments tend to arise over differing interpretations of some event: you both feel that you're "right," and you are. However, you are each "right" in the context of your personal backgrounds and experiences. That does not make you objectively correct. Once you've reached *that* understanding, the ideas in this book help to fill in the actions/behaviors to enable you to live peacefully with your partner—at least until the next upset.

Because some people have such strong views about the "rightness" of their knowledge and ways of working in the world, they prefer to work by themselves. They may have trouble working in group settings. Others prefer to solve problems in a group and have difficulty when asked to work alone; without leadership, they may not know what to do.

Similarly, some people like to take personal responsibility for the results of their work while others prefer to share responsibility for any project or task. Blending these two, some people prefer to work with other people while maintaining sole responsibility for a task. They're in charge, but not alone.

This is what makes a horse race.

Ascertaining whether you're speaking with a solo-thinker or a group-thinker (or some blend of the two) helps you understand the other person's language of work preferences. The more you know about how the other person thinks and works, the easier it is to speak in the language (and symbols) they understand.

This is a chapter that explores some core beliefs and assumptions. This has to do with how you react in the world. Here are some related quotes:

- Just because you feel bad doesn't necessarily mean someone did something wrong.

- Just because you feel good doesn't necessarily mean what you're doing is right.

- Expectation on your part does not incur an obligation on someone else's part.

- If you're afraid to say it, that means you need to say it (or it will diminish some aspect of you or your relationship).

- Different people express love differently; learn to recognize the way others express and receive love.

- Don't treat people the way you'd have them treat you; treat them the way they'd have you treat them.

- Pay attention.

Chapter Three
Personal Variables

Most communication glitches arise from differences between the way **you** see the world around you based on your own upbringing and life experiences from the way the person with whom you're communicating sees the world around **them** based on *their* upbringing and life experiences. Taken together, your past has created the way you are today: your past confines you to your current reality.

This chapter takes a stab at teasing out some of the areas that influence your reaction to things people say to you. We'll touch on the following four topics:

- Love
- Beliefs
- Thinking
- Upsets

When you discuss these topics with others—whether or not your full-time partner—I believe you'll be surprised both by how similar and how different their views are from yours. As I've been mentioning, differences in background and upbringing produce adults with very distinctive opinions/views that affect communication success or failure. It's not that one of you is more "right" or "wrong" than the other, just different; you're simply not aligned. Being more aligned generally results in smoother communication. Translation: these are topics you may want to learn to understand about yourself and your Significant Other.

Love

For years, this topic has been beaten to death in relationship self-help books and magazines. I'm not going to do that. This brief section is intended to broaden your views about the concept of "love" in order to increase your awareness of communication subtleties when emotional issues arise about your relationship.

Aspects of Love
How the Greeks saw it
In a very general way, the Greeks viewed "love" as a triangle with three points. Each person's "love" was some blend of these elements. The particular mix of romantic love, friendship, and flat-out *choice* gave each relationship its own particular characteristics.

- **Eros**—love based on passionate devotion (this usually means sex)

- **Philia**—a brotherly affection, generally non-sexual

- **Agape**—the love that brings forth caring, regardless of circumstance (love by choice; spiritual love—pronounced ah-**gah**-pay)

Storge, a fourth aspect of love according to the Greek philosophers, refers to the kind of affection felt by parents for offspring. For the purposes of illustrating my point, I'd like to leave *storge* aside and concentrate on *eros, Philia,* and *agape.*

This material is relevant, because those in relationships may not feel pulled towards the same kind of love as their partners. Differences can lead to hurt feelings. Some would describe their feelings for their partner as a combination of *eros* and *agape*, while others might describe it closer to a combination of *Philia* and *eros* with some *agape* thrown in. Think of your love as some point within the triangle encompassing all three types of love. Your partner is also at some point within the triangle. The closer together you and your partner on to describing where you land on this triangle, the closer you are to having the same type of feelings (love) for the other.

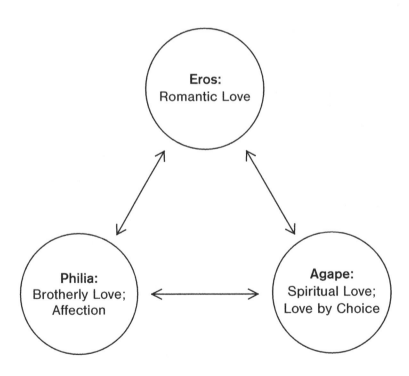

Obviously, this is another area where couples can benefit from thinking about and discussing the kind of love they feel towards one another (and the purpose of their relationship).

Permit me to make a few additional comments. It can be risky to wallow in romantic love (*eros*)—even though it's a lot of fun and feels good. *Eros* is usually thought of as fleeting. In modern English, *eros* is really a euphemism for the kind of emotions referred to as *new relationship energy* (NRE). Conventional wisdom says emotional connection at this level lasts about three months. Some have called this stage *The Three-Month Crazies*. Those who require *eros* to feel comfortable in a relationship purposefully and slowly dole out new experiences in an effort to extend the *Three-Month Crazies* and ride the NRE wave as long as possible. People who go from relationship to relationship are thriving from the NRE and may find it very, very hard to break that cycle and settle down with one person.

Obviously, stable relationships depend both on liking and loving your partner. *Philia* means loving friendship. People who think about such topics assert that by first developing *philia* and then blending it with *eros*, a couple can more naturally meet their partner's needs while concurrently fulfilling their own.

This model is threatened by violating the bonds either of love or of friendship. In fact, because *philia* is *close loving friendship*, breaking trust at this level (through dishonesty, poor integrity, or disloyalty) frequently breaks the tie with romantic love. This occurs because violating the trust of friendship by someone who supposedly loves you can become an unforgivable hurt.

Agape describes one's love of the spirit within another person or, more broadly, within God. *Agape* is reached through the intellect: one evaluates a person or concept and makes a choice to love them/it.

I'm spending time describing *love* in this detail because it may help you to more effectively communicate your wants and needs for each other (and for the relationship) once you can clarify how you feel about one another.

To Love vs. To Be In Love

Think of it this way: you love your children, but you're not in love with them. You love your parents, but you're not in love with them. In relationships, it happens sometimes that one of you loves the other, whereas that other is *in love* with you. This subtle difference can cause conflict and upset unless this issue is clear to each person.

The emotional states of *loving* or being *in love* are not black or white issues. One is not an objectively better emotional state than the other. The challenge arises when one expects to be *in love,* yet finds that while they *love* their partner, the *in love* aspect is missing. Often, people in this situation think something is wrong and needs to be fixed. We are asserting that *loving* is not a less powerful emotion than being *in love*—the defining action is your willingness to commit love your partner without the romantic being as prominent as it was previously.

In psychology, the "love vs. in love" scale is referred to as a "scale of emotional involvement." Obviously, people in relationships have various levels of emotional attachment. For some, other factors (such as financial need) outweigh the need for emotional connection. Whether emotional attachment is important in the relationship depends upon a person's *motivations* for being in the relationship.

Motivations

While most pairings result from great sexual chemistry, not all relationships are sex-based. People have their own reasons for starting and remaining in relationships. I know a man who chose his partner because he wanted help changing some personal habits that he knew she wouldn't tolerate. I know a woman who picked out her guy because she wanted to be treated like a little girl (literally). I know a gay man who married a lesbian so they each had "social cover" in our heterosexually-biased culture. I could go on, but so could you.

The message is this: people may not understand important motivations that cause them to pick a certain partner. They may *think* they know why they want that person as a partner, but to outsiders, their answer may not ring true.

Ask yourself: What motivates you to seek (or remain in) this relationship? What does this person offer you that you'd have trouble finding in someone else? Are you staying with this person out of a sense of duty? If so, who said it was your duty?

If you're in a relationship, you may wish to discuss the kind of love you offer one another. Perhaps more important, you might wish to explore what each of you has to do so the other person recognizes and feels your love for them.

Conclusion: motivations influence communication. Communication is what holds the relationship together.

Intentions

While some communication is casual and filled with small talk, other communications (particularly work-related) are influenced by the speakers' intentions. Here, the question is whether you and your listener are discussing the same thing for the same reasons.

First example: Two of you are focused on solving a problem. Your intentions are aligned, and you're getting a lot done. Suddenly, one of you realizes the time: their intention abruptly changes from helping to solve the problem to finding a graceful way to leave. Conversation quality degrades.

Second example: It's after work. You and your partner are at home. Customarily, this is the time when you reconnect emotionally by sharing about your workday. However, today you'd rather not talk about your day, so you're not fully engaging. Actually, you think you should start preparing your partner about some serious work-related problems, but you're afraid of their reaction. So, you are not quite listening to what your partner is saying, and you're not being very direct in what you're saying about your day. Your partner senses that something is wrong, but can't figure it out because you're being evasive. In self-defense, your partner erects emotional barriers. The rest of the evening is a disaster.

Two factors affect the quality of your relationship: the *intention* you hold within your relationship and the quality of your interpersonal communication. It's worth digging in and having serious discussions to discover whether the two of you are in the relationship for the same reasons. Intention is the key to all of your relationship actions—including communication.

Beliefs

The process of clarifying your values opens a door to your motivations and behavior. Your parents and early education largely set your values: today, they affect the way you think, communicate, and treat others. If your parents were lucid and had a large vocabulary, chances are you do, too. If they were poor communicators, chances are you are, too (unless you've worked very hard to overcome that patterning).

People get satisfaction when they live in accordance with their values. Conversely, people notice when their lives are *not* aligned with their values. For example, if you are stuck all day in an office but you really value fresh air and physical exercise, you're going to wish you could change jobs. If you value clear communication but find you're interacting with people who hide their emotions and disguise their intentions, you're going to notice your own discomfort.

In a few pages, I've provided a list of value-words. Considering the extent to which values affect your beliefs and behaviors, you may want to spend a little time actually digging below the superficial meaning of these words to explain exactly what it means to *you*.

Definitions of most value-words depend upon your belief system, your worldview. Don't be surprised to find that others have quite different interpretations and reactions to the same value-word. These differences should be instructive—in subtle and also in obvious ways—as you and others have different backgrounds.

As you begin this exercise by reading the value-words, you have to get past your initial reaction to say something like: "Equality—yes, I definitely believe in equality." Take this challenge seriously: ask yourself probing questions aimed at finding the heart of each value. Don't try to get away with "yes/no" answers. Explain, expand, and discuss: be thoughtful:

- Does one of you feel that the other is of equal value or of lesser value as a person? Why do you feel this way?

- Does the man consider himself to have greater value in the relationship because of his role as husband/father/protector?

- Does the woman consider herself to have greater value as the mother and nurturer of the family?

- Do you believe that all men are equal, or is there a hierarchy?

- Do you treat as equals those who have been in a relationship for five years but have never read a book on relationships?

- Do you treat as equals the grocery store clerk, the bank teller, and the homeless person?

- How do you express your feelings of equality?

This is actually a very challenging process. Not many people are willing to go through it on their own or with their partner. However, you will benefit from it: you will come to know yourself better.

(Note: When deriving relationship-level values, you'll want equal input from your partner. You'll need to work together to reach conclusions about the meanings and relevance of these words as values you hold as a couple.)

Before you review the list, I've selected three words and suggested some questions to help guide you as you develop your own questions for other topics on the list. The words are:

- Accountability,
- Change, and
- Values

Accountability, Change, and Values
You might at first think it odd to link accountability, change, and values: let me explain. One changes throughout life. As your values develop and mature, the way you are in the world also changes. To point out the obvious, the person with whom you started a relationship X years ago isn't the same person with whom you're now living. You've both changed in uncountable ways. But, this is where accountability and values come into play. As some people get older, they become more autonomous: they are less accountable to others. However, as other people get older, they become more dependent on others—more accountable for their actions and time.

So here's a question: did they ask you if they could change? Did you ask them if you could change? Are there certain levels of change that would need to be "cleared" by your partner? Is there someone else (family member?) to whom you are accountable should you wish to make a large change in your life?

Even in two paragraphs you can see how accountability and change can be linked—but there are other major variables. For example, your own relationship with "change" has a strong influence on how roughly or smoothly you transition through change.

- Do you seek or resist change? Why? What background/history surrounds change for you?

- At a small level, will you consider changing from one task to another before the first task is complete? (This is a powerful question, because the way you do one thing is the way you do *all* things. You may have to read that sentence twice. It is one of life's profound truths.)

- Do you view *change* as a mental rejuvenation or as threatening in some way? In what ways threatening?

- What value do you put on change?

Now, this last bullet brings up the last major aspect of change that I'll cover: your values. Your values affect both how much you care about some topic (such as *communication* as an abstract concept) and also what you say to people and how you react to what people say to you.

I've included an abbreviated list of value words. You might wish to make a copy of these words and mark those that are your top 10 values. Number them. Have your partner do the same (not seeing your choices). By comparing results, I think you'll find some insights that will help you better understand your relationship with accountability and change.

List of Selected Values

Accomplishment
  vs. success

Accountability

Accuracy
  vs. getting it done

Adventuresome
  vs. reclusive

Challenge;
  solver vs. follower

Change
  vs. status quo

Cleanliness
  vs. orderliness

Collaboration
  vs. working alone

Commitment;
  to a cause, to people

Communication;
  essential vs. selective

Concern for others,
  empathy

Continuous improvement
  vs. organic learning

Contentment
  vs. satisfaction

Cooperation
  vs. working alone

Creativity;
  its role in your life

Decisiveness
  vs. leaving wiggle room

Discipline
  vs. correction

Efficiency;
  alone, vs. effectiveness

Equality

Ethics;
  situational vs. objective

Excellence
  vs. doing an okay job

Fairness

Faith
  vs. proven conclusions

Family
  vs. work vs. hobbies

Freedom

Friendship

Fun
  vs. growth experiences

Goodness

Gratitude

Hard work
  vs. cleverness

Harmony,
  in relationships and life

Honesty

Honor;
  bestowed vs. earned

Independence

Inner peace,
  calm, quietude

Integrity

Justice

Knowledge;
  nice to know vs. driven
  to know

Knowing
  vs. understanding

Leadership;
  natural vs. learned

Love;
  in love vs. to love

Loyalty—
  how is it broken?

Merit
  vs. seniority

Money,
  donating to causes

Money,
  having and use of

Openness;
  candor vs. diplomacy

Peace,
  non-violence

Perfection,
  attention to details

Personal growth,
  in relationship structure

Pleasure,
  sources of

Positive outlook;
  half full vs. half empty

Practicality
  vs. dreaming

Privacy
  vs. full disclosure

Prosperity and wealth—
what can money buy?

Reliability
vs. accuracy

Resourcefulness

Respect for others

Results-oriented
vs. process-oriented

Safety,
physical, financial,
social, etc.

Satisfying others

Security,
physical, emotional,
financial, etc.

Self-givingness,
restrictions on, etc.

Self-reliance;
dependence vs.
independence

Service,
to others, society

Simplicity
vs. complexity

Skill
vs. luck

Spirit in life

Stability

Status

Strength

Succeed,
a will to

Success,
achievement

Systemization
vs. dynamic, changing

Teamwork vs. solo work

Time,
concept and value of

Tolerance,
toward others and self

Tradition;
past vs. new

Tranquility

Trust

Truth;
subjective vs. objective

Unity

Variety

Wisdom

This material affords you the opportunity to explore a world of little doorways into yourself and your partner. I believe you will better understand your own motivations after working through this list.

If you are in a relationship, working through this list may reveal a range of new possibilities to explore. Communication within your relationship will improve to the extent that you understand your partner's values. You each have goals, and together, these goals support the intent and purpose of your relationship. In that light, you strengthen your understanding of one another (and stabilize your relationship) when you work toward mutually derived goals. Anyway, "working toward your goals" gives you something to do at night other than watch television.

By the way, there's a risk in losing sight of your goals: your relationship may drift. It may drift from your initial intentions, goals, and dreams, and end up swallowed by the routines of everyday life. As with most things in life, it's more difficult to retrieve something that has left you than it is to keep it from going away in the first place. It's the same here; it's easier to keep your relationship on track through good communication and goal-setting than it is to rebuild it after you've drifted apart emotionally.

Applying Values to Your Life
While the first step towards change involves identifying your key values, the second step involves translating those values to action. Here's a brief example. This is really material you have to do on your own.

Thinking

Assumptions

There are some large-scale assumptions that underlie discussions about *communication*. Here are three "quickies":

- Your mind doesn't distinguish between what *really* happened and the way you've *reconstructed* the event as having happened. Thus, unless you are a skilled observer, your version of reality is pretty much just your own version of reality.

- Jungian *projection* causes you to contaminate your interpretation of events. You project what **you** would mean if you said/did "X" onto the person saying/doing "X" and then react to it. (We'll spend more time on Jungian projection in Chapter 4.)

- You make what is referred to as *the usual error.* "The usual error" is your belief that other people think (or problem-solve) as you do.

Keeping those three assumptions in mind, here's the most general overview I know of about the consequences of communication:

Something happens → realities get set by both parties → meanings get assigned.

People can react to events in unusual ways. If you do "X" and get an unexpected response, there's a good chance they are reacting to unknown and unresolved personal issues having little or nothing to do with you. In fact, it's quite possible this person's emotional baggage has just taken over your conversation.

Value	What do I want to happen?	What am I going to do about it?
Having a close family	• I don't want us to argue over my smoking • I want us to enjoy time together as a family • I want to be able to give my kids reasonable amounts of spending money • I want my family to feel proud of me	• Stick to my resolution not to smoke • Not smoking with improve the quality of our time together • Tricky...spending less on cigarettes will help • I will make realistic commitments and keep them
Being competent	• I want to feel more competent in my work • I want to feel less pressure to be perfect all the time	• I will commit to taking classes/courses in my field • Learn to accept that I'm fallible by disputing the belief that I have to be marvelous at everything
Being emotionally stable	I want to have better emotional control	I will learn and practice skills for handling feelings, particularly those that sneak up on me

While I don't mean to sound melodramatic, you might wish to think about this person as *not quite in their right mind*. Their thinking may be a little irrational. In extreme cases, you may find you're saying "A," "B," and "C" while they are responding to "stone," "K," and "hay." It's at this point that you, being on the receiving end, must be very, very careful not to further trigger this situation.

Here's the kind of conversation you want to avoid. You're in the heat of a really bad emotional meltdown. One person says: "Fine, we're done!" The listener takes this to mean the relationship is over and says: "Fine!" They gather a few belongings and leave. The first person is in astonished shock. They didn't want their partner to go; they only meant the conversation was over. The person leaving didn't really want to go, but they thought they were told to get out. There you are; both people are fuming and hurt. A mess.

Heated communications can lead to odd outcomes neither person wants. It's not that one or the other person was at fault, exactly. When two people blend their energies, they create a new entity called "the relationship." It has its own distinct energy pattern with unique challenges and opportunities. It also has its own set of communication rules. It can take a long time to figure out what they are.

IQ and Work Experiences

Ummmm. This one is going to be a little sensitive. The issues concern your "crunching power" (raw IQ), and working styles. (Thinking styles—as opposed to working styles—are touched on in next section.)

In my experience, higher IQ doesn't mean a person has more *information* than someone with lower IQ, but it does usually mean they have faster access to what they know. I've also noticed that high-IQ folks can string a number of disjointed bits of information together to reach more interesting conclusions than the rest of us.

Extreme IQ differences can affect a relationship because each person has developed work styles that fit their IQ. This is not a bad thing, it's just that large IQ differences can create relationship stress and upsets if not handled carefully.

For example, the higher-IQ partner may become frustrated that the lower-IQ partner can't problem-solve as quickly as they'd like, or has trouble combining diverse bits of information to see the big picture. If this applies to your relationship, then I'll throw in a comment made by T. H. White: "The most difficult thing in the world is to know how to do something and to watch somebody else do it wrong, without comment." (*The Godstone and the Blackymor,*1959 p.161.)

Message: both of you will be stressed by little things that come up when IQ differences are more than 20 points or so apart. You will both be served by remembering that alternate problem-solving approaches aren't necessarily *wrong*, they're simply *different*. Learn the strengths of your partner and agree to "let go" of your *way* of doing something when that something is within their strength field. Your IQ may be higher, your crunching power may be quicker, but they may have technical skills that are better than yours. An important relationship lesson is to *get out of the way* so your partner can serve you using their strengths.

In my experience, IQ and working styles (learned as a function of prior work experiences and training) can intertwine and have a huge impact on a relationship.

Thinking Styles

Your thinking and working styles influence your communication preferences—and your communication preferences influence your working preferences. For example, if you are an introvert with *guarded* communication preferences, your working style is likely to differ from someone who is an extrovert with *lucid and transparent* communication preferences. Again: one is not better or worse, but knowing your own thinking and working styles helps you to control yourself when working with others.

As I'm not a psychologist, I'll keep this section short and send you off to do more exploring on your own. I'm going to take a couple of cuts at this topic.

Taking a very broad view, are *linear thinkers* (people who tend to go from A to B to C to D) are quite different from those who are *branch thinkers* (people who go from "A" to "stone" to "zebra" to "X1.") This can be either very good or very bad. If you and the person with whom you are speaking are starting with the same "A" but you are reaching a *better* "X" (say, "X1"), then branch thinking is working for you. On the other hand, if you're starting at the same "A" and ending up with "*library*" rather than "X1," then it's probably not so much that you're using branch thinking, as you aren't in control of the way you problem-solve. You've ended up in a logic set that is not part of the alphabet. I actually lived with someone with this trait; I was always caught off guard when she came up with a *related* conclusion, just not a conclusion that I thought I wanted or needed.

We don't need to control our partner's thinking style, but we need to be able to discuss their conclusions and determine which conclusions to or not to follow and explain *our* reasoning to them.

Sometimes we get caught up in trying to figure out **how** they think and miss the spectacular conclusions they're offering us. Often, more than one possible path is revealed when two (or more) people involved in the decision-making process. It's great if we both get to "X" or "X1"! However, if one of us gets to "X" and the other get to "library," maybe we need to do "X" in the "library." Let's talk about this different conclusion and make a joint decision.

Great books in these areas include:

- *Lateral Thinking: Creativity Step by Step*. Edward DeBono, Reissued 2015 [DeBono has a number of books out on *thinking,* e.g.: Six Action Shoes.]

- *Thinking Better*. David Lewis and James Greene, 1985

- *The Ideal Problem Solver*. John D. Bransford and Barry S. Stein, 1993

- *Teaching Thinking Skills: Theory and Practice*. Joan Boykoff Baron and Robert J. Sternberg, 1986

Now: The way you think also affects how well you get along with those who are listening to you. It's a matter of rapport. People get along best with people who think like them. Large differences in thinking styles can doom a relationship: I know of more than one such case. If one member of a team just doesn't "get it," they will be singled out and isolated by other team members. A person's thinking style goes to the core of that person's being. How you think (and how you deal with those who don't think like you) is a major interpersonal issue.

Harrison and Bramson (*The Art of Thinking*) found that there are five distinct thinking styles in Western society. I'm particularly fond of this book because their descriptions of these thinking styles—and ways of working with people who think in each of these patterns—are so pragmatic and helpful.

Harrison and Bramson found that most people prefer one or two of *inquiry modes*:

- The *synthesist* sees likeness in apparent opposites. They are interested in change.

- The *idealist* welcomes a broad range of views and seeks ideal solutions.

- The *pragmatist* seeks the shortest route to payoff. Their motto is: "Whatever works."

- The *analyst* is looking for the "one best way" and is interested in scientific solutions.

- The *realist* relies on facts and expert opinions. They are interested in concrete results.

These basic thinking styles are strongly influenced by the thinker's fundamental beliefs (back to "worldview"). These beliefs channel people to think about things in a restricted way. To use contemporary examples, it's hard for most Americans to understand the logic and viewpoints of radical Islamists or the leaders of North Korea.

In their book, the authors give everyday examples to produce a hands-on guide to teach you how to unbind your mind from narrow thinking. This is useful, yes? After all, who wants to be accused of thinking narrowly?! Seriously, though: this is important material. Your ability to communicate clearly with someone depends to a large extent on whether you are able to interpret and understand *their* thinking style.

The Art of Thinking is intended to help you select effective strategies for asking questions, making decisions, getting along with people, and solving problems. By learning why you think the way you do—and understanding thinking styles of others—you should be better able to get past obstacles and turn conflict into cooperation.

This next subsection provides another cut at the *thinking* topic.

Distorted Thinking Patterns (cognitive distortions)

This material has been adapted from *Feeling Good: The New Mood Therapy Revised and Updated* by David D. Burns, 2008. I liked this book: these ten bullet points helped me to see *thinking problems* that come up in everyday speech. Forewarned is forearmed, and such.

- *All-or-nothing thinking:* Things are presented in black-and-white terms. If part of a performance falls short of perfect, the entire performance is seen as a failure. (This is the "throwing the baby out with the bathwater" syndrome: "Okay, you don't like the way I cook rice, I'll never cook rice for you again.")

- *Overgeneralization:* A single negative event is seen as part of a never-ending pattern of defeat. ("Tell me, are there *any times* you'll believe what I say without verifying it?")

- *Mental filter:* The person picks out a single negative defeat and dwells on it. Over time, their vision of reality becomes darkened, like the drop of ink that colors an entire beaker of water.

- *Disqualifying the positive:* The person insists that some positive experience "doesn't count" for some reason or other. They dismiss positive experiences in order to maintain a negative belief that is contradicted by everyday experiences. (e.g.: Despite others thinking the person is competent, the person maintains they are not competent.)

- *Jumping to conclusions:* The person makes a negative interpretation of a situation without objective facts to support their conclusion. Here are three examples:

  ○ Mind reading. The person arbitrarily concludes that someone is reacting negatively to them, yet they didn't bother to check this out.

  ○ Projection. The person projects personal beliefs, behaviors, fears, or insecurities onto another person, then reacts to them. (This is a common and pervasive problem that bears a lot of thought and attention. We discuss Jungian projection in depth a bit later in this book.)

  ○ Fortune telling. The person anticipates that things will turn out badly, and then feels convinced that their (unrecognized) prediction is already an established fact—and reacts to it that way.

- *Magnification, catastrophizing, and minimization:* The person exaggerates the importance of things (such as a personal "oops" or someone else's achievement), or they inappropriately shrink things until they appear tiny (their own desirable qualities, for example).

- *Emotional reasoning:* The person assumes that their negative emotions reflect the way things really are: "I feel it; therefore, it must be true." (Note: in the language of Transactional Analysis, this is the "child voice" speaking. It's full of emotional words and change in vocal pitch and tonality.)

- *Should statements:* The person tries to motivate him/herself with shoulds and shouldn'ts. It's as if they have to be whipped and punished before they can be expected to do anything. "Musts" and "oughts" are in the same category. *Guilt* is the emotional consequence of this kind of ongoing self-punishment. When someone directs *should* statements towards others, the reaction is usually one of anger and resentment. (Note: in the language of Transactional Analysis, this is the "parent voice" speaking.)

- *Labeling and mislabeling:* These are extreme forms of overgeneralization. Instead of describing their error, they attach a negative label to themselves: "I'm a loser." When someone else's behavior rubs such a person the wrong way, they will attach a negative label to them: "They're a &%#@." Mislabeling involves describing an event with language that is highly colored and emotionally loaded. (Note: in the language of Transactional Analysis, this is another example of the "child voice" speaking.)

- *Personalization:* The person sees themselves as the cause of some negative external event that really had little or nothing to do with them. (The modern saying: "Don't take things personally, it's not about you" is the counter-position.)

To the extent that you can identify distorted thinking patterns in yourself and others, you can work to expose the faulty logic. People who repeatedly think with these patterns often have self-image issues, so it may not be easy to stop them from thinking this way. However, if you can, it will help the person develop a stronger sense of self.

Working Styles

Do you know how you prefer to work? Do you mostly enjoy thinking up ideas or implementing ideas? Do you mostly enjoy research or are you a stickler for detail work? Put in the language of social psychology, where are your strengths?

- As a *fact finder?*
- Good at *follow through?*
- As a *quick start?* or
- As an *implementer?*

There is an online assessment that does a very good job of identifying your working styles. It's called the "Kolbe A" index, and it's easily found by an Internet search. The Kolbe A Index measures a person's instinctive method of operation, and identifies ways they will be most productive. Test results show how you score in four dimensions: quick start, implementer, researcher, or follow-through. This information helps you understand your own strengths and those of others who have taken the test. At work, this information helps you choose the kinds of jobs that are most suitable for you and those you should probably avoid. In relationships, if the two (or more) of you take the test, you'll see how your various strengths mesh or collide. I highly recommend this test.

Yes, there is a modest cost. Yes, it's worth it.

I'm also a big fan of the Myers/Briggs Type Indicator assessment. It has helped me to understand my partner(s) and myself (and also my work colleagues: our HR department had everyone profiled).

According to their website: "The purpose of the Myers-Briggs Type Indicator® (MBTI®) personality inventory is to make the theory of psychological types described by C. G. Jung understandable and useful in people's lives. The essence of the theory is that much seemingly random variation in the behavior is actually quite orderly and consistent, being due to basic differences in the ways individuals prefer to use their perception and judgment." Differences in behavior result from basic differences in the ways individuals prefer to use their perception and judgment.

Perception involves becoming aware of things, people, happenings, or ideas. *Judgment* involves the ways we reach conclusions about what we've perceived.

The Myers/Briggs model is based on the premise that if people differ systematically in what they perceive and in how they reach conclusions, then you should be able to predict their interests, reactions, values, motivations, and skills. It turns out they were right.

Ultimately, Myers and Briggs described 16 distinctive personality types that result from combinations of the various possible judgment/perceptions preferences. In a general way, here are the variables:

- World view: introvert (I) or extrovert (E)

- Managing information: deal with facts (S) or interpret and add meaning (N)

- Decisions: look at logic and consistency (T) or at the people and special circumstances (F)

- Structure: in dealing with the outside world, prefer to get things decided and closed (J) or stay open to new information/options (P)

Once the test has revealed your preferred ways of interacting with the world, your *personality type* is expressed as a four-letter code. Mine, for example, is INTJ. In all, there are 16 personality types. You can learn to adapt your own communication strategies (and even the ways you approach someone) by learning about the interaction between your Myers-Briggs personality type and the personality type of the other person. This gives you a HUGE advantage in crafting clear and effective communication styles.

I'm impressed with the test's accuracy. It has given me insights that improved my communications/relations with people in general and specifically with those for whom I know their Myers-Briggs profile. The following three books provide the keys to understanding yourself, how you'll work with others for whom you know their Myers/Briggs score, and interacting at work.

- *Please Understand Me: character and temperament types* (David Keirsey and Marilyn Bates)

- *Please Understand Me II: temperament character intelligence* (David Keirsey)

- *Type Talk at Work: how the 16 personality types determine your success on the job* (Otto Groeger, with Janet M. Thuesen and Hile Rutledge)

I've found this the least expensive way to get an outstanding personality analysis.

Upsets

Here's how upsets occur: Something happens. The brain of the party decoding that "something" makes interpretations and assumptions and builds a "story" that enables them to understand what they think they saw/heard happen. Ah! They now have a memory of what happened! However, there is a slim chance their interpretation of this event was objectively accurate, because it hit this person's filters and interpretations and became transformed into something different. (By the way, wars come from this kind of misinterpretation of events.)

Anyway, the person whose body is attached to that brain reacts to their understanding of what happened. Depending upon how closely that person's brain was able to correctly interpret the event, their response is both reasonable and logical, or rather misses the mark.

Some couples experience upsets with nearly every verbal exchange. Each person is twisting the words or intent of the other and the result is called "an upset." These snafus have to be addressed or they become part of the relationship's downward spiral.

I once heard it said: "Temper gets you into trouble; pride keeps you there." How you handle upsets speaks volumes about your personal self-control. This section is designed to give you some options when you encounter situations that stir you up.

"Being Upset" vs. "Having an Upset"

In 1975, I went through a training course called *est* (lower case intended). That stood for *Erhard Seminars Training,* and it still exists as *The Landmark Education Forum.* There, I learned a distinction that's had a profound impact on my life. They made the distinction between "being upset" and "having an upset." They pointed out that the phrase "I am upset" describes (and reinforces) your emotional state of being upset. By stating you are upset, you are declaring that you are not fully in control of yourself.

Worse, you're now *at the effect* of being upset; your emotions have run off with you. In a sense, your rational self has been hijacked. There are consequences for losing control of your emotional self. The person toward whom you are upset or angry can use the opportunity to manipulate you because you're being controlled by your emotions. This is not a good position to be in.

"All of our anger and frustration is self-induced. The world might invite us to be upset, but we choose to accept the invitation." (Source unknown.)

Stopping an Upset

To avoid being disarmed when upset, you can teach yourself to do *pattern interrupts*. This is a concept from NLP (Neuro-Linguistic Programming) and discussed extensively in most Tony Robbins' self-empowerment programs. The moment you sense you are getting angry, change your (emotional) state. Stand up. Sit down. Stretch. Take three deep breaths. Go get a drink of water. *DO* something different than you've been doing. Change your physical position as a way of buying time to get control over your emotional state. If you can stop the process of becoming angry and get control of yourself, you can then learn to **choose** your reaction. This isn't an overnight fix, but it suggests a path for gaining better self-control.

To help you choose your reaction, think about how you can be the cause of your reaction, rather than being at the effect of your anger. Translation: Choose to *have an upset*. This is something like choosing to *have* an ice cream cone. In the same way you can choose to have a chocolate or vanilla ice cream cone, you can learn to choose whether you will or will NOT have an upset. (Hint: Just before you're about to explode, you will sense some physical sensation in your body. In my own case, the back of my scalp starts to tingle. This provides only a second or two to act to change my response to my triggered reaction. However, a second or two is **plenty** of time to change your emotional state.)

You are going to have to make up your own method of breaking the action-reaction cycle to turn it into an action-action cycle. Ultimately, you are responsible both for your actions and reactions. This applies equally to your partner.

Master your state and you'll sharply reduce the unexpected explosions and upsets common to every relationship. Ask yourself: why are you even bothering with this upset? What's your motivation? Do you want the problem to stop recurring or do you only want to stop the person from being upset?

A suggestion: Recognize upsets in order to stop them. Make a pact with your partner: both of you agree to recognize when one or both of you are *choosing* to have an upset, rather than *being* upset. This helps reinforce each of you for making this change from the way you've previously handled unsettling situations.

Causes of Upsets

Nope, I'm not a psychologist, but I've gone through a lot of personal therapy and reading in an effort to get better control of myself. So: what do you think causes most upsets? Actually, it's a pretty concise list:

- Once upon a time something happened. You were embarrassed. You were offended. You resented it. However, you couldn't do anything about it. Now, when similar issues arise, you react by being upset. When you feel you are more distressed than you think you should be under these conditions, chances are you've just landed on top of your emotional baggage. The remedy is to let go of the trigger; let go of the situation causing you to relive the upset. Unfortunately, it may take a good deal of therapy to identify the root cause.

- *Homo Sapiens,* as wild creatures, had to watch out for threatening situations. Whether it concerns tasting a new food or meeting people not quite like us, modern-day Americans have this bias towards caution. Unfortunately, it can lead us to be suspicious and emotionally closed to unknown experiences. You can gain greater control over your own reactions to new people and situations by adopting more of an observer view. Enforce detachment. For readers who want to go further down this path, it's the path of forgiveness and patience laced with the practice of daily gratitude.

- Some people nourish their upsets and resentments daily. They've made them into lifelong friends. They wouldn't know quite how to go through the day if they weren't constantly bitching about something. For those of you who listen to *Prairie Home Companion,* the way Garrison Keillor's "mother" speaks to him provides a great example. If he says something is good, she finds ways to show it's not good at all. In fact, it's really bad. If he doesn't call her as often as she wishes, she heaps buckets of shame and mortification on him. Unhappiness is her life. My father's mother was like that.

In my experience, you can convert bumpy upsets into more even fields by learning to disengage emotionally and to view the occurrence (whatever it is) as a one-off "phenomenon." Stop feeding it with your personal story. Destroy the loop that says once "A" is triggered, B, C, D, E, F, and G have to follow.

They don't have to follow; you're letting them follow. Stop it!

Remember: Tom Miller's audio CD program *Self-Discipline and Emotional Control* can help you learn how to stop your runaway emotions.

Managing Upsets with Compassion

Okay: your partner/colleague experienced strong emotional reactions to something. You blew up. It wasn't trivial or the exploding person wouldn't have risked revealing that side of themselves. It's tough to regain composure quickly in order to manage such a situation with grace. One option, of course, is to call Grace. Grace usually likes to be welcomed with Gratitude. While you're sitting in your warm apartment or home having an emotional meltdown, consider where you are, really.

Really, you're in the United States. You have adequate housing and food, you're safe from predators, there is a good health-care system, and you are probably earning money at a job. Statistically, you're in a very small percentage of the world population. According to the United Nations Development Programme's "Human Development Report" of July, 2014, fully 50% of the world's population live on less than $2.50 per day, and 80% live on less than $10 a day. 22,000 children die daily as a direct result of poverty. Something like 1.1 billion people have inadequate access to water. It's pretty sobering.

Next time you or your partner hit an emotional landmine, you might reflect on those numbers and hug one another. Go out for a cup of coffee.

Once you've learned methods for converting upsets from an emotional to a thinking state, there are some strategies you can use to improve the overall outcome:

- Recognize and honor their emotional reaction. (e.g., "I understand X has upset you.").

- Express compassion instead of judgment. Express understanding; show appreciation instead of criticism. (e.g., "I see now how this has upset you and I appreciate your willingness to express your emotions in front of me.").

- Demonstrate willingness to change instead of blaming them. (e.g., "I apologize if something I said triggered you; can we talk about this and learn from it?").

- Offer reassurance instead of shame. (e.g., "Know that I cherish you and we can work out ways so this does not happen again.").

- Express acceptance instead of guilt. Most emotional outbursts result from the perception of a breach of trust. (One usually learns to accept the message(s) hidden in upsets and use them in a positive way. However, to the extent you, <u>yourself</u> become reactive in this setting and say hurtful things that make your listener feel guilty, the relationship will be wounded.)

- Demonstrate curiosity instead of making them wrong. (e.g., "What just happened? What's led up to this upset?" Great leaders lead with questions.).

Recognize that *Upsets* Generate False Memories

Like historians and novelists, we construe our own histories as we see them. Our version of past events creates our reality. Here's how it works. Something happens. We simultaneously assess and interpret what happened. We assign meaning to the event, categorize its importance, and draw conclusions. We identify what we will do and what we will not do about the event. We then form lingering opinions. This melding (or collapse) between *what happened* and the *meaning we assign to it* occurs in an instant. Objective memory of what "really" happened disappears in a flash, and we're left only with our reconstruction of what happened as seen through the filters of our lives.

The thing of it is, what objectively happened and how we subjectively remember what happened are two independent and separate occurrences. Our subjective version of whatever happened becomes the stuff and story of our lives. We can spice up or water down our stories. We tell the long or short version; we add drama or subtlety. The kind of story you tell depends upon your archetype. Warriors tell stories of aggression and battle; victims tell stories of being used. Regardless of how clever we are or how different we believe the circumstances to be, what continually emerges is pretty much what we've previously experienced: we're in a loop. While we might believe our stories are new, it usually turns out there are only two or three basic themes repeatedly playing themselves out, often in ingenious ways.

Our stories represent the richness of what it means to be human. There is a power, validity, and value in them. However, you'll want to keep your background stories from spoiling your present life. This brings us to what we might call the downside of stories: our interpretations keep us stuck. Without thought, we overlay our stories on current events and put a spin on almost everything that happens to us.

It may help to break such loops when you realize the stories we tell are only our interpretation of events and are no more true or false than another interpretation.

I don't want to keep going along these lines, for this is not a philosophy/psychology book.

If you're interested in exploring ways of interrupting your reactive/revisionist actions after upsets, I (for the third time) recommend Tom Miller's audio course: *Self-Discipline and Emotional Control.* Here is a four-line summary of what he teaches you to understand and to control:

- emotions are always real;

- they come from your horse (often called your "monkey brain");

- but, they are not your emotions;

- it's what your horse has created as the reason things are done a certain way.

Miller's material is about the: "When you did X, I feel Y because I made it mean Z" loop. This is an extremely powerful course and not for the faint of heart. He uses strong language: actually, he yells at you. As he points out, that's about the only way to get through to your horse (monkey brain).

Seven Keys to Communication Success: Good Habits

- Be a bright light: go out of your way to spread lightness and happiness. Avoid speaking ill of anyone.

- Listen in neutral: listen to what others say without judgments. Avoid getting caught up in their stories (their version of events).

- Know who you are. Understand your own standards and respect that others live by different standards. Theirs are simply different from yours, neither better nor worse. Our daily behavior expresses our unique interpretations of our experiences. When people with widely different backgrounds are speaking, the door to miscommunication is opened.

- Be outwardly optimistic (regardless of how you may actually feel): look at the glass as half-full. Concentrate on looking for the good in all people and situations. You can make a project out of this and force yourself to be optimistic.

- Be proactive: when you see something amiss, step up and participate. Be the example others follow.

- Take responsibility for repercussions resulting from your actions, whether large or small: own your role in the situation. This is a core leadership characteristic.

- Although you believe your own opinions are facts, such is not always the case. Your opinions can trick you when you least expect it. Remember: you can only know what you can remember, and memory is outrageously fickle. You tend to remember things in ways that favor the preservation of your self-image.

Chapter Four
Emotional Challenges

Bad acts in a relationship can help you calibrate to what you will and will not accept. Bad acts help set ethical boundaries.

Harsh words leave wounds; dishonesty breaks trust. In some cases, broken trust can never again be fully restored and you live with a person whom you fundamentally distrust.

Hurt people hurt people.

When someone has their feelings hurt, they tend to strike out to hurt the other person. This can create an escalating loop of unhappiness and discomfort. Depending on the depth of the wounding, one or both people will begin to disengage emotionally. The passionate and loving feelings that brought you together become a foggy, distant memory. In your upset reality, you're not happy and you're not sure what to do about it.

Sometimes, when you're both upset, the best you can do is to agree not to do more harm.

The role of emotions in communication could easily become a book in its own right. To keep this manageable, I've selected only four topics. I've selected these because they represent a range of emotional issues that influence your communication with others. Some of the ideas, tips, and techniques should help you work through challenging times that arise in work or home relationships.

Section headings:

- Emotional issues
- Personal issues
- Relationship issues
- Fears

Managing Emotional Issues

Recent research suggests that the effects of stress differ between men and women. Researchers determined stressed males tend to act more egocentrically and are less able to distinguish their own emotions and intentions from those of other people. On the other hand, stressed women exhibit a nearly opposite reaction: they become more prosocial. That is, they exhibit behavior that is positive, helpful, and intended to promote social acceptance and friendship.

In lay terms, this means that stressed men tend to become defensive and aggressive, while stressed women tend to become nurturing as they work to de-escalate the situation. This bit of information is relevant for your communication style when stress is building up between you and someone else.

Emotional Styles

In a general way, six factors determine emotional style. Our response to people and events represents a mix of how we manage the following qualities. If you're going to work on yourself beyond reading the words in this book, each of these six areas represent major areas ripe for personal introspection and change.

- *Resilience:* How quickly can you recover emotional equilibrium after an upset? A very resilient person more easily shrugs off stressful situations, or more quickly finds ways of coming to terms with what happened.

- *Outlook on life:* This is a "half-full glass" or "half-empty glass" issue? Said more formally, where you fall on the optimist-pessimist continuum affects your emotional style.

- *Sensitivity to context:* This quality has two parts. First, whether you have the skills to adjust your behavior when a dynamic situation changes; second, whether you have the skills to control your emotional state and your languaging (the way you use your words) when a conversation suddenly moves into emotionally dangerous territory.

- *Social intuition:* Social intuition concerns your ability to recognize social cues such as body language, facial, and verbal expressions.

- *Self-awareness:* How good are you at grasping signals from your own body and mind? Self-awareness includes physical sensations, emotions, feelings, thoughts, instincts, and intuitions.

- *Attention:* This quality concerns your ability to focus upon a conversation, task, or situation. Attention is an aspect of *mindfulness.* If distracted, can you manage distractions and pull your attention back to the task-at-hand?

While there are lots of ways people respond to an emotional punch, common reactions are:

- To punch back emotionally. Raise your voice; raise the stakes; threaten.

- To clam up. You won't talk about it right then (or ever). You may not know what to say or do to improve the crisis, so you leave it alone. Many people will leave the room in order to process the hurt privately.

- To drop into some form of stylized speech pattern that indicates you're going through old emotional loops and feeling threatened by this current emotional outburst.

Your maturity in handling personal stress or pain (or stress/pain that you cause another) is an important aspect mastering your self-control an adult. Clearly, it's also critical in your role to maintain a stable relationship, whether at home or at work.

Four Elements of Emotional Control
Stripped to the bare essentials, the simplest formula for handling an emotional upset has four components:

- Stop your immediate reaction to the situation,
- Disconnect from it,
- Honestly explore what just happened, and then
- Start speaking with the other person to flatten the issue.

Stop your immediate reaction the situation: The first step in stopping emotional communication exchanges is to recognize your role and your listener's role in the exchange. In my experience, one of the simplest and most effective techniques for doing that is called Transactional Analysis (TA). Transactional

analysis looks at verbal exchanges as transactions represent-
ing what they call one's "ego state." They identify three ego
states: parent-like, childlike, or adult-like. Their thesis is that
the words one uses when speaking help yourself and others
understand the mutual behavior.

Because I discuss TA under "therapeutic listening" in Chapter
Five, I'll only mention now that you have it within your power
to switch from child-child or parent-child self-perpetuating and
emotion-laden upsets to adult-adult discussions that deesca-
late the situation.

As with most communication tools, it takes some practice even
though it's not difficult.

Disconnect from the situation: People seem to fall into one of
two general camps: either they like to work through emotional
issues when they arise or they specifically want to avoid con-
tinuing discussions over emotionally touchy topics until they
can regain control of their own emotions. People in this second
camp are particularly concerned about saying something rash
that further damages the relationship.

I'll go over some solution-seeking strategies in the final chapter. Those will include techniques you can use once the two of
you are ready to bring up the cause of the emotional conflict.

Explore causes: In the Army, you're taught to perform an "After-
Action Review" (AAR) whether the "situation" went will or went
poorly. It's a quality management-and-control issue. While you
can look up the Military's format, the simple civilian version
just asks just a few basic questions:

- What happened?
- Why did it happen?
- What needs to be done so it does or doesn't happen again?
- What positive lessons did we learn from the experience?

Flatten prior issues: "There's baggage and there's luggage. You take ownership of the luggage and you're working on it." Jaime Nichols, private discussion 2016.

Baggage leads to surprises. Surprises seldom help a relationship, whether it's a relationship with someone at work, a friend, or your domestic partner. Although it happens all the time in life, it's not fair to others: they shouldn't have to deal with your emotional baggage in addition to their own. Similarly, it's not fair that you treat your current partner the way you learned to treat a prior partner. After all, if you went into a restaurant and the waiter presented you with a bill just as you sat down, you'd object. "It's not my bill: this was the last diner's bill" you'd say. "I know," the waiter would reply, "but the people at this table didn't pay their bill, so now it's yours if you want to eat at this restaurant."

You'd get up and walk out. (Analogy originally told to me by Richard Moore, 2015)

However, you stay in relationships where your partner is presenting you with "bills" unresolved from their past. Not fair. Right? But, who said life was fair?

Just realize what you're dealing with and why it may be hard to change someone's reactions. They didn't settle their bill before moving in with you. They may not have known about the bill as their partner ran up the charge.

Tip: You can use a stylized response structure to help reveal hidden messages. I'll discuss it again in about thirty pages in the section titled "Clarity of your Speech." It goes like this: "When you said (or did) 'X' I took that to mean 'Y.'" People often speak or act assuming that their speech or actions are clear and obvious to others. That's not always so. By providing feedback that communicates how YOU understood what someone said or did fosters clear communication. When the person with whom you're speaking understands what you took their communication to mean, they then know whether or not you heard what they intended to say. Sometimes the speaker's message/actions were unclear; other times the hearer's baggage altered the intended message.

People have all kinds of different relationships with their life experiences. Some people hold on to their past hurts because they don't quite know what to do with themselves without these past hurts to explain why they're so stuck in life.

Other people keep careful track of hurts caused by those close to them and throw them back when the opportunity presents itself–often as they're leaving the relationship.

Still others have learned how to change their own reactions to past upsets: they have learned to dissolve and release unpleasant memories. We can take back our emotions by revisiting/retelling the stories or interpretation of the prior acts/actions. Perhaps the most common method is to reimagine the story but to give the story a happy ending. Done often enough, they can diffuse the emotional power behind the experience. Now, the outcome no longer upsets them. This is a sophisticated and priceless tool, and I pass it on to you.

Regardless of the way you manage your emotional history, your own mental health depends on being able to stay in the present without being haunted by a past you cannot alter.

By the way, some issues are harder to flatten than others. Some issues involve broken trust. When *trust* is involved, you may want to explore the concept of atonement. The offending person proposes some "atonement options" and they negotiate a resolution. Once again, this is a subject you'll have to explore if it interests you.

Now: the discussion we've been having for the last few pages assumes that you've engaged with the other person and communicating about some impassioned issue. However, some people (usually but not always the person in the less-dominant role) may not react to an emotional provocation. Instead, they "stuff" their own views or opinions: they don't say them out loud. That's probably not emotionally healthy.

Don't "Stuff" Your Feelings
Some people stuff their responses because speaking them will escalate the already-difficult situation; others stuff their responses because they are working or living in a structure where their views are disregarded (so why bother saying them).

Stuffed emotions will come out at some point; some little thing will set them off. Often, the triggering incident is an emotional landmine. An emotional landmine is an issue hidden from both people that causes a huge upset once triggered. This overreaction may upset both people: the person who triggered the upset may be both astonished and apologetic; the person experiencing it is reliving past trauma of some kind.

Emotional explosions frequently occur because underlying issues were not addressed when they first arose, often years earlier or in a prior relationship. Perhaps they weren't addressed because the person couldn't identify *what* to address. Typically, "stuffing" is a psychological self-defense mechanism learned in childhood. It may even have mostly succeeded for a while. However, carried into adulthood, emotional stuffing works against those attempting to establish and maintain a close and intimate bond with others. Yes, stuffing may avoid conflict, but it also prevents you from constructively working through the underlying issues.

This is not a case of, "What you see is what you get," it's more like: "What you see is NOT what you have."

Unconditional Love

Expressing unconditional love for someone is a separate discussion from liking that person. You may love your partner but not like what they're doing right now.

So, let's talk about this a bit.

The phrase "unconditional love" expresses the conceptual opposite of *conditional love,* love that must be earned and maintained. With unconditional love, love is given freely to the loved one no matter what. Unconditional love endeavors to separate the individual from their behaviors and excuses the loved one from any threat of loss-of-love due to their bad behavior.

Unconditional love is different than unconditional dedication. Unconditional dedication (or *duty*) refers to an act of will irrespective of feelings. For example, a person may feel a duty to stay with an aged parent or a minor child even though they don't like that person.

Unconditional love has both a positive and a negative side.

On the positive side, showering someone with unconditional love supports them to become the person they want to be rather than someone you or others think they should be. Additionally, by distinguishing between love and behavior, you become open to the possibility of speaking with them about changing some of their behavior without invalidating them as an individual. This enables the other person to feel the emotional safety of knowing they are loved and valued, even when they make mistakes.

At least fairly minor mistakes.

On the negative side, if the person you loved unconditionally takes advantage of that love (or behaves in ways you find ethically or morally wrong), you may choose to love them in theory but not have them in your life. After all, everyone is responsible for what they make out of their lives. Occasionally you'll find that people you have loved now behave in ways that exceed your tolerance. Sometimes it's best for your own self-preservation to let them go.

Personal Issues

Obviously, all kinds of personal issues influence your communication skills and abilities. Some people have more common sense than others; some people have had a more challenging childhood than others. In this section, I'm just grabbing a few often-hidden topics to go over with you.

This section is divided into the following parts:

- Subcultural differences
- Self-image
- Childhood hurts
- Projection
- Priorities
- How you view failure
- Orderliness vs. cleanliness

Subculture Differences

Your adult values reflect the values of the subculture in which you were raised. Think of someone raised in a gang-riddled inner-city vs. someone raised in a neighborhood filled with first-generation Vietnamese youth. Conversely, think of someone raised on an Indian reservation and then someone raised in an exclusive area of Beverly Hills, California. Adult values develop differently in these settings. In some cases, the community values toughness and macho aggression. In other cases, the community values hard work, study, and education. In still other cases, people are judged on their poise, dress, and erudite speech.

As children grow to adults, they adopt many of their parent's views about such things as:

- Power vs. authority;

- Worth of an individual;

- Value of strong family ties;

- Skill of tolerating ambiguity or uncertainty;

- Ability to handle stressful personal interactions with skill and empathy;

- The extent children are expected to be self-sufficient vs. being helped through life by a tight-knit community;

- And so on...

Communication is not restricted to conversation, of course. You communicate a world of information by how you hold yourself, how you walk, and how you speak. Some people are taught these skills as children. Their parents taught them how to walk and speak with authority and to stand erect and with controlled breathing from their diaphragm. You can often pick out people who have grown up with wealth and education, not only by their clothing accessories (*subtlety* counts; *flashy* detracts) but also by their walking style (clearly purposeful and unhurried). I vividly recall being at the end of a fairly long backpack trip with my then-wife and my father in the late 1970s. As we hiked out of the Maroon Bells (Aspen area), we passed a man walking towards us. I didn't notice him at all, but after he passed, my father noted that he had no idea who that man was, but he was clearly a Man of Wealth and Power. Without going into my personal background, my father would have been taught to recognize such a person.

Consider choosing a way that you both can walk and speak to convey what you want others to believe about you. Consider the look of your home. Using little more than your imaginations and interesting interior decorating, you can create your own fantasy world and move right in.

[Note: I am sitting on a leather couch with my computer on my lap. There is a fire in the fireplace and I'm wearing a smoking jacket and ascot. My evening shoes are black suede loafers. A DVD is playing the sounds of a thunderstorm on one of our sound systems. The other sound system is playing shamanic music. All the lights are dimmed and the artwork is lit individually. No television. We each have our own fantasies: mine are just mine. And, I'm eccentric.]

By way of applying what I've been saying, sometimes background differences augment your relationship, sometimes not so much. Low-grade friction may disguise the real issue: what one person takes for granted surprises the other. Such misalignments can be hard to pinpoint. You're blind to most of your own behaviors because they are so much a part of you. You make what is called: "The Usual Error." The usual error is to think that others think like you. (See: *The Usual Error: Why we don't understand each other and 34 ways to make it better* by Pace and Kyeli, 2008)

People don't think like you. Your background, values, and experiences color every conscious moment. Without video documentation, there is very little chance that two people interviewed 30 minutes after having a discussion (let alone having an argument) would describe the same event. Close, perhaps, but little details would have changed.

By the way, this is why the person taking meeting notes largely defines what was said and accomplished. They wrote it down (through their own filters of understanding).

Self-Image

Few people see themselves as others see them: a truism, to be sure. Even within your circle of friends, you know people who are extremely emotionally stable and who have high self-esteem, and you know people who have very low self-esteem and whose drama-filled lives play out for everyone to see.

Now: A person can have emotional or social issues that are not particularly visible. They have learned how to "fake-it" until something in the relationship stresses them. While New Relationship Energy will blind one partner to oddities in the other, warts and wrinkles aren't so easily dismissed after some months together. Problems arise. Trouble starts. The way people react at this stage is strongly influenced by the way they have developed coping skills to deal with a chaotic upbringing. Here's a story...

A researcher was interviewing adult children of alcoholic parents. They conducted separate interviews of brothers who were three years apart in age. One of the men was an alcoholic; the other was not. Each man was asked about their drinking habits. One brother said: "I wouldn't touch the stuff, just look what it did to my parents." The other brother said: "Of course I'm a drunk. Who wouldn't be with parents like that!" Even people raised with very similar backgrounds draw quite different life-lessons that affect their future. People develop different coping skills to deal with a chaotic upbringing.

Obviously, one's self-image is made up of lots of variables. Here are few that are pretty self-evident, they're here only to make sure we're on the same page in order to go deeper:

- *Lovability:* lovable/unlovable continuum;

- *Ego sorting:* seeks or does not seek opportunities to help others;

- *Worth:* worthy/unworthy continuum;

- *Competence:* generally effective in most tasks, or generally ineffective in most tasks;

- *Outlook on life:* half-full or half-empty glass (or expecting someone else to fill it); and

- *How they know they've done a good job:* internal/external validation. (That is: Are they satisfied that they did a good job because they planned and completed it successfully? Or, do they need approval/recognition from others to feel satisfied that it was a good job?)

As this isn't a textbook, I'll stop. My point is that when the couple is interested in personal growth, they need to know quite a bit about one another. Much of this book explores ideas to help you to know your partner more thoroughly.

I've just listed some of the obvious areas where one's outlook can affect a relationship; here are some of the unobvious areas.

Childhood Hurts

By nature, humans are on the lookout for "bad things." We tend to remember them and build up defenses against them. Researchers refer to this tendency toward caution as "negativity bias." It's been bred into us since we were cavemen. Life back then was so risky that only the cautious survived.

Now let's consider personal memory. Bad things happened in all our childhoods. Our parents, neighbors, and their friends may not have considered them to be bad but our child-brains interpreted them that way. We developed strategies to deal with our perceived threats. Most strategies were reasonable and logical; some weren't. To this day, you may have unexplainable reactions to certain events: "X" happens and you produce reaction "Y."

Defensive reactions developed in childhood often create behavior patterns that can be triggered as an adult. If you or your partner reacts automatically to certain situations in surprising ways, chances are there are some buried landmines lingering about. The problem is, you're no longer in situations where those are helpful, and now they are (potentially) harming your relationship. Here are some examples of ways childhood reactions have played out in adulthood.

- I know a woman whose sexuality is tied to being spanked or to spanking. This person recognized that she was getting sexual stimulation from spanking by the time she was four. Because "being spanked by my parents" would have been interpreted by her child-mind as "having sex with my parents," this person went to great lengths to be the perfect child, always doing more than was called for and being an outstanding student.

- I know a lady whose upbringing was so harsh and brutal that she learned to lie and be deceptive in all her dealings. She also had learned how to disguise these core traits, but every so often they bubbled to the surface. In my view, there was no possible way to help her.

- I know a person who told me that his entire life was changed when he was in his mid-20s after hearing a single exchange from the movie "Harvey" (Jimmy Stewart, 1950 remade in 1998). He quoted it to me and I wrote it down. The quote was, "Years ago my mother used to say to me, she'd say, 'In this world, Elwood, you must be'—she always called me Elwood— 'In this world, Elwood, you must be oh so smart or oh so pleasant.' Well, for years I was smart. I recommend pleasant. You may quote me."

  This person said that he spent many years going to therapists and workshops in order to change his outward persona from being "Oh so smart" to being "Oh, so pleasant." I thought he had done a remarkable job.

Smooth relationships depend upon both partners understanding one another's motivations and dreams. A person who hides this knowledge from the other is controlling the relationship. More explicitly, the emotionally closed person (the person keeping personal secrets) controls the relationship by not matching the emotional risk level of the other partner.

Chances are it won't last. I'm speaking from experience.

Jungian Projection
This topic is well known; it's easy to find good information about it. The key concept is that people frequently project their private fears and insecurities onto those close to them and then react. Often, Person A is really mad at themselves and Person B can't make sense out of the anger.

For example, let's say that you (yourself) have a pattern of leaving tasks incomplete. You're a dilettante and you know it. It's a weakness in yourself that has bothered you for years. Now, you've asked your partner to do something. However, the way they are doing it differs from the way YOU would do it. Rather than asking them why they are approaching the task in such a way, you jump to the conclusion that they are not going to complete the task as you wished. You become reactive. You are likely to end up in an upset. Actually, you have projected your own annoyance at *your own* inability to complete tasks onto your partner and reacted against yourself. Your stunned partner doesn't understand any of this. They only understand that you've lashed out against them for doing exactly what you'd asked them to do.

Not all people solve the same problem in the same way. We're back to "The Usual Error:" assuming that others think as you do.

Now, it gets worse. These cycles often feed off of themselves. For example, if your partner has abandonment issues (broken home, spouse left without notice), they might interpret some of their partner's actions as precursors to **their** leaving. This can lead the "accused party" to start to withdraw emotionally for self-protection. This—in turn—may cause the "accusing party" to reciprocate the withdrawal process even though they started it. Neither person understands what just happened: the scene has gone from "person 'A' asking person 'B' to do task 'X'" to an emotional meltdown. Landmines. Triggers. Big Red Buttons.

If the wounded party had simply mentioned their concerns directly with their partner, that partner may well have said,

"What? I've always behaved that way; it has nothing to do with you at all. It's just the way I was brought up."

Which is why I wrote—and why you're reading—this communications book. Most of these conflicts can be disarmed if you'll recognize them and talk about them.

Priorities

Here are some questions to help you think about priorities. These questions are meant to help you determine whether both of you place the same importance on something. While these questions are all strung together in a few paragraphs, each requires serious thinking and discussion with your Significant Other.

- Do you organize your life to get the most done in the least amount of time? Do you even care about efficiency and effectiveness?

- Are you able to prioritize your life to maximize growth and achievement? What does "growth and achievement" mean to you? Do you care about these areas? If you do, how do you make "growth and achievement" real and measurable?

- Do you spend quality time discussing your career and family challenges with one another? Do you try to minimize emotional conflict? Have you prepared yourself to have those crucial conversations that are so necessary when you feel your partner is not being honest about their actions, feelings, or concerns?

- Do you make time to release stress and free yourself from everyday worries and anxieties? Do you allocate enough high-quality personal time to build positive memories with one another? How do you build memories together: do you build memories in the same way? How much time per week do you watch television? What could you be doing to enrich your relationship if you weren't watching TV?

- Do you have adequate help at home? Does one of you need to get a second job?

"Soapbox stuff," you scoff.

"Too much work," you mutter.

It takes constant work to communicate successfully with others. Successful communicators stand out in all settings.

Orderliness vs. Cleanliness

I'm going to bring this up—briefly—as it's been a particular issue in my own life. With my Asperger Syndrome, I care more that the house is tidy and orderly looking than whether the carpets have been vacuumed or the kitchen floor mopped. Personally, an orderly house is a *need* and a clean house is a *want*. This can lead me to spend quite a bit of time tidying up when my partner would prefer that I come to bed.

I realize that Asperger Syndrome is an unusual condition, so few readers are going to resonate with this issue. However, people have all kinds of idiosyncrasies. Most of us are relatively normal; others of us are somewhat eccentric. In my opinion, relationships benefit from some in-depth discussions about personal preferences and where they fall on the "wants vs. needs" continuum.

Financial Issues

I suspect that money issues cause most of the friction and emotional trauma among couples. As I see it, this topic has five friction-related components. They're worth reviewing, as friction affects stress and stress affects clear communication:

- There simply isn't enough money;

- One partner has MUCH more money than the other;

- One partner has very different spending habits than the other;

- One or both of you feels trapped, no easy way to leave;

- You're not married but are living together: one partner declines to create any legal documents for emergency situations (health or financial).

This topic really does not require much elaboration; everyone gets stressed when income doesn't cover expenses. I have no particular insights into this problem, and everyone reading this book knows the common answers. You can use a tightly controlled budget; you can start preparing to get a better paying job. Of course, one or both of you can start working a second job, but then you're likely to see additional friction mount over the scarcity of time you can spend together. This is certainly a challenge.

There Simply isn't Enough Money

Many people find themselves without enough money to cover their basic expenses. This happens because the economy changes, because you lack education or training, or because of age or medical conditions. These are all familiar issues with

well-known solutions. You can take distance-learning courses; you can read and study more about your field; you can
join networking groups; you can stop watching TV and start
exercising. Importantly, you can change your mental relationship with the concept of money and wealth. That path is well
described by people writing about "The Law of Attraction."
(You might start with the book: *What to Say When You Talk to
Yourself* by Shad Helmstetter, 1990. That will start the change
process from the inside out.)

Financial Imbalance Between Partners
In some relationships, one person (usually the woman) essentially surrenders financial control to the other. It's nothing
formal; we live in a patriarchal culture where men are expected
to run the financial side of the relationship. Sometimes that
works out well, sometimes it doesn't. Anyway, not all relationships follow that norm.

There is a palpable fear of letting go of one's financial safety.
I get it. This is particularly true when one person has far more
assets than the other. How does it work if one of you is worth,
say, half a mil and the other person has about $5k to their
name? What if one person has a long history of financial management and the other has none? I'm not here to prescribe
answers; I'm here only to highlight areas that may underlie
some hidden concerns, fears, or anxieties that will affect your
ability to communicate cleanly with your partner.

People who have grown up far above or far below the average
U.S. norm probably exhibit behaviors invisible to themselves
that stand out when interacting with people with more average
upbringing. Despite best intentions, these differences can
make others uncomfortable.

For example, some people who have grown up amidst wealth may (subtly) assume they're entitled to the special or preferential treatment. Others (particularly with substantial education or business background) may assume they are naturally better prepared to lead the relationship (or conversation) and are intolerant of opposing viewpoints. People tend to notice those who have grown up with what are euphemistically called "expectations." If you find yourself thinking, "She acts like such a snob," or "He's so condescending," you've just experienced someone expressing their entitlement attitudes.

When there is a large asset gap between people, it can cause the person with the greater assets to speak and act differently than if the assets or incomes were closely balanced. I know one couple where the man had no assets to speak of (and a very modest income) while the woman had substantial wealth and didn't work because of outside income. She handled all financial decisions—usually without consultation. After some years, the man found himself in a new job. He now earned enough to support the family. His wife commented to me that the day he took that job, he announced that he now intended to be much more involved with financial decisions and budget control. I silently noted that their financial imbalance must have been an unrecognized stress-point that he had never been willing to discuss.

Feeling Trapped

I'd guess that one or both partners in most personal relationships feels financially trapped. After all, it commonly takes both people's incomes/assets to support your lifestyle. One will do what one must when financially entangled. This includes putting up with a lot of bad behavior from the other person. You may wish to consider establishing separate emergency funds, funds wholly in each of your names. Personally, I'd recommend establishing dedicated savings accounts to hold six months of living expenses plus moving and resettlement costs.

Financial independence goes a long way toward giving you a voice in any discussion. You won't fear the consequences of speaking *truth* at work or at home.

Personal Spending Habits

Differences in spending habits can become annoying. In a work setting, you may find a colleague who buys pretty much whatever they want and talks a lot about spending money. This can lead others to want to demonstrate their own value by speaking about their personal strong suits. This tit-for-tat retaliation can lead a less affluent person to disclose more personal information than they should. This stems from their effort to maintain social balance. It won't work. It draws attention to the fact that they changed the subject.

In a relationship (particularly one not bound by marital rules), friction can develop when one person can dip into their independent assets to buy pretty much what they want but not offer the same freedom to their partner. This may be a good discussion topic if only one person in the relationship has to watch their expenses. Imbalance within a partnership (whether a work or a domestic partnership) speaks to a person's values and beliefs. People with similar values and beliefs are likely to be able to build a smooth relationship.

If *money* is a hot topic in your relationship, you might want to plan ways to manage the discussion. You'll not want to appear to be challenging. For example, the two of you might want to explore how money is symbolic for each of you, what your beliefs are about money, and how to honor each other's financial concerns in the case one of you loses their job (for example). Break the large topics into their smaller parts and work through each one. The discussion is pretty much over if your partner becomes defensive.

However, if they become defensive, you now have useful information.

Emergency Provisions

Discussing contingency plans gives each of you the opportunity to raise personally important issues. The way discussions develop can affirm or threaten trust between partners. On the positive side, financial and emotional candor can help to ease abandonment fears by demonstrating trust. You can help drive off the dragons of imagination by planning for a variety of financial, medical, and relationship crises. This is particularly true for aging couples who might be facing complicated medical issues.

Emergencies bring stress. Preparation eases stress. An emergency is bad enough: you can at least prepare to the extent that you've written down and shared information about where to find key medical, financial, and family information.

Surprises happen. Case in point: In 2006, I had a nearly fatal heart attack. It was a week after moving in with my former partner. Nothing was in place for emergencies. I arrived at the hospital and didn't even have my medications list. I learned a lot from that experience: my meds list is in my wallet and my partner has a current list of all my passwords. I've prepared a document titled, "If I am dead or hospitalized" and placed it as the first document listed in my "My Documents" folder on my computer. On my cellphone, my home screen is blank except for a single "Note" icon. Opening that icon directs you to the document on my computer.

It's pretty easy to prepare for "normal accidents." The key is to work with your partner to document important areas of your lives. In a general way, here are areas to discuss. We've included a list titled "Preparing for 'normal accidents'" in the supplementary material at the end of this book.

- Is your cellphone set up to help first responders know whom to call if you can't speak? Are all your doctors (and their specialties) listed on your phone with the last name "Doctor" so they're grouped together for First Responders to find? Is your medications list in your purse/wallet?

- Do you have funds set aside for an emergency? Can your partner access that money? Are your bank accounts joint? Do you have a certain amount of cash on hand in your home? Does your partner know how to find it?

- Do you have Powers of Attorney established for medical necessity? How about DNR (Do Not Resuscitate) orders? Living will?

Honesty issues

It can be scary to be honest. It can be a relief to be honest. It can hurt to be honest.

But, what does "honest" mean? My guess is that it doesn't mean exactly the same thing to your business or relationship partner as it means to you. Part of the challenge of writing about "honesty" within a specific relationship is that people have somewhat different views about whether an act (or a failure to act) represents dishonesty in the context of their particular relationship. For many, "honesty" can be influenced by the particular set of circumstances occurring at a particular time. (Situational honesty is a sub-set of situational ethics and beyond the scope of this book. Those using *situational ethics* believe outcomes—rather than the rules—justify the way you do things.)

Nonetheless, *honesty* has boundaries and limits that have evolved from your values. As I've already discussed, your values developed from your upbringing, experiences, and education. As with many things in life, "honesty" has some subjective qualities to it.

Consider: when asked, "How was your day?" your partner certainly does not expect you to take the next eight hours to provide a minute-by-minute recital. When a work colleague asks, "Hi, how are you today?" they really don't want an answer that requires real interaction. Actually, they don't want to hear anything negative.

So: how much honesty do you want from your partner, and *vice versa*? I know some couples who want lots of details about their partner's day; I know some couples who really don't care what their partner does when they're not together.

You have to develop your own acceptable limits and expectations about honesty as it relates to integrity and trust. And, if you're seeking harmony in your relationship, your partner has to understand (and agree) with your limits.

But that's theory and now we'll get down to practice.

In my experience, personal honesty and integrity thrive when people have a solid and happy relationship based on mutual respect. It thrives when both people feel that life with their partner (or their work) is interesting and personally fulfilling.

When something changes in the dynamic and those warm fuzzy feelings start to go away, there is a human tendency to put up walls of emotional protection. If one person starts to question the other person's commitment to the relationship, red flags of warning start to unfurl. Remember what I said very early in this book: If you're not working on your relationship, you're really not *in* the relationship. People can tell when their partner isn't as "in" the relationship as before.

Dishonesty is invited to the table when one person's behavior changes in ways they can't explain to their partner's satisfaction. Trouble *really* starts if one person's *wants* are being met at the sacrifice of their partner's actual physical, medical, or psychological *needs*.

There are three areas where *honesty* comes up:

- Acts of omission and commission
- Lying
- Willful opposition

Acts of Omission and Commission

An act of commission is doing something that you know you should not do. An act of omission is NOT doing something that you know you should do. In work or in personal relationships, most people view omission and commission as equal trust violations. They represent failures to protect the other person's feelings.

Failing to protect your partner's trust can be deadly in a relationship. My partner, Jen, puts it this way: "Imagine *trust* as a fresh sheet of paper. Think of *broken trust* as that piece of paper being crumpled. Even if you iron the crumpled paper, it will never again look new. Your word is your bond and it is all you have in this world; be careful how you pledge your word."

In my own view, you have daily opportunities to practice living up to your word: drive the speed limit—it's part of your Social Compact. Be places when you say you'll be there—you've given your word. The more you are able to keep your word on small issues, the more easily you'll find it to keep your word on large issues. You'll have developed the habit of being reliable.

As they each represent dishonesty, continued acts of commission or omission can be grounds for ending a relationship. If serious enough, one single act may separate a couple, even after many years together. As an example, I have a friend whose wife of 28 years filed for divorce the moment she discovered he'd had an outside affair. I'm sure you know couples where the same thing has happened.

Lying

In a general sense, lying is a cooperative act. You can only be lied to if you (subconsciously) agree to the lie. Sometimes you can be deceived against your will. This sounded like an interesting topic, so I've read some books about it. I recommend two of them to you:

- *Never be Lied to Again: How to get the truth in 5 minutes or less in any conversation or situation* by David J. Liberman, 1999, and

- *What Every BODY is Saying: An Ex-FBI Agent's Guide to Speed-Reading People* by Joe Navarro and Marvin Karlins, 2008.

Here are some of the key points from Liberman's book (I'll be mentioning some more about Navarro's book in a few pages.)

- On any given day, you can be lied to anywhere from 10-200 times;

- Strangers lie 3 times in the first 10 minutes of meeting each other;

- We lie more to strangers than to co-workers;

- Extroverts lie more than introverts;

- Men lie 8 times more about themselves than about other people;

- Women lie more to protect other people;

- Within a married relationship, you lie one out of every 10 interactions; and

- If you're unmarried, you lie one out of every 3 interactions.

Our culture sanctions lying. It's hereditary. Babies will fake a cry, pause, wait to see what happens, then go right back to crying.

- One-year-olds learn about concealment;

- Two-year-olds bluff;

- Five-year-olds lie outright and manipulate through flattery;

- Nine-year-olds are masters of cover-ups; and

- By the time you reach college, you're going to lie to your mother in one out of every five interactions.

As adults, we live in a "post-truth" society. Just think about it:

- Spam;

- Fake digital friends;

- Fake Facebook accounts;

- Partisan media who now use "fact-checkers" to separate truths from untruths after major speeches and political ads;

- Ingenious identity thieves; and

- World-class Ponzi schemers.

The general message is this: Everyone can be deceived for something they hunger for. So: the question becomes, how can you spot a liar? (This applies to a non-professional liar. Someone who lies for a living won't be easy to spot—they know how to overcome these tells.)

Lying and body language

There is an art to reading body language. It is a topic that lends itself to study and practice. I've summarized a few common observations that the pros use to help them assess a suspect's truthfulness. Bear in mind, while these guidelines apply to amateur lie-tellers, not professionals. People who depend upon dishonesty for their livelihood know all about this and have practiced not to give these signals.

Unusual body movements: Body language will change slightly when a normally truthful person starts telling a lie. Their breathing pattern may change, too. It may get deeper louder: you may even start to hear them breathe. You also may see unusual or oddly-timed posture shifts. In some cases, their body will start looking defensive: shoulders pulled up and elbows pulled more into their sides.

Hand movements: Those who are normally honest may express their own anxiety over their unethical behavior through hand movements. They may clench their fists to keep their hands from moving or (at the other extreme) fidget a lot with their hands while speaking.

Voice pitch: A person's vocal pitch tends to go higher when lying. This happens when a person's larynx tightens as anxiety causes all their body muscles to tighten. A tightened larynx causes the higher pitched voice. This also happens when a person raises their voice: the shouting is in a higher pitch. Again, this is related to their overall tenseness tightening their larynx.

Covering the mouth or fiddling with their face: Sometimes, even intentional liars forget to monitor these nearly-instinctual behaviors. Supposedly, this happens because their sub-conscious mind wants to avoid telling the lie, and covering part of their face represents a symbolic hiding.

Unusual pauses or delays in responses: The speech of a liar may involve unusual pauses as they work on creative answers to your questions. Thinking about the story they are making up takes time and concentration, so, watch out for unusual breaks in a liar's speech. By the way, the liar may become agitated/angry as a reaction to feeling trapped. They are likely to try to turn the tables by becoming verbally aggressive with you in order to regain conversational control.

How to tell if someone is lying

Just let them speak. Don't interrupt. Usually, liars over explain in an effort to tell their fabricated story. However, here are some other tactics you can use if you want to toy with your victim.

- Try changing the topic and see how easily the liar will be ready to change the subject. The liar's body and face will look relaxed (rather than confused) because they're holding it in a relaxed state as part of their theatrical delivery.

- If you think you're getting false answers to your questions, probe for details. As previously mentioned, you'll likely hear a pause as the liar tries to imagine how what they have already said fits into the new situation you've just asked about.

- Wait some time. Hours or days. Then, return to the suspected lie and again ask probing details. Most liars will have different answers, because an imaginary story is difficult to remember. The liar is likely to become flustered and defensive as you point out discrepancies in the stories.

- If you are able to look directly into the person's eyes as they are speaking, you'll be able to catch slight changes in eye-movements connected with the story you're challenging.

Anyway, if the person with whom you're speaking is lying to you, you're well along the path of broken trust, so you're probably protecting yourself by erecting emotional walls. Lying, of course, represents a character flaw. Few of us will encourage a relationship with someone who cannot be trusted.

Willful opposition?

If one or the other person in a relationship is willfully opposing the other, they're sending a message. You'll want to open that message and understand it. Chances are, one person's willful opposition has triggered the other person, and neither of you are very interested in discussing what happened. Personally, I'd say that you don't have that luxury. You need to know what's going on. (Unless, of course, you've already decided the relationship is over.)

One reason you'll want to find out what's going on is that nothing may be going on. You may be imagining the whole thing. Remember our discussion about *projection*? One of you may be misinterpreting the actions of the other. That's why communication is so important.

Let me tease this apart for a moment.

People solve problems in ways that work for them but may not make much sense to those watching. My first partner (of 17 years) was like this. I could never quite figure out why she did certain things along the way to her final solution. I found that I was much calmer when I studiously avoided observing her problem-solving processes.

In a work setting, there are two general approaches that people take when managing someone who is completing a task for them. One approach takes the *macro* (large-scale, visionary) view of task-management; another takes the *micro* (small scale, detailed) view.

With macromanagement, the person assigning the task leaves the person alone with it. They expect the person to complete it in their own way.

In contrast, a micromanager wants to retain control. They want to find out *how* this person solves problems. They may become concerned about the way a problem is being solved, and may monitor the person doing the work

While constant micromanagement may wear you out and annoy your partner, it can be a useful tool to learn about their working and thinking styles in order to establish (or re-establish) trust in their judgment. Often, micromanagement provides that information.

Here are two examples of these management approaches. The task is to get you both to a meeting in a different city over a specific weekend.

As a **micromanager**, you may give broad parameters about ticket costs or the type of hotel, but basically, you just want the task completed. You may assume that your partner will be cost-conscious, but beyond that, you leave them alone.

As a **micromanager**, a task assignment is accompanied with a discussion of the important variables, such as:

- Optimum ticket price;
- Particular airports at each end (if relevant);
- Seat preferences;
- Frequent flyer account numbers;
- Hotel preferences, especially hotel club memberships;
- Special room requests;
- Proximity of hotel to meeting location;
- Rental car with GPS;
- Weather check;
- And so forth.

This focuses your partner on your travel preferences. They are not to do anything to the travel plans that you have not stipulated. Once the task is completed, you may ask some questions:

- Any challenges?

- How were they resolved?

- What additional resources were needed to complete this assignment (travel agent, Internet research, a particular airline's reservation system)?

- How long did the process take?

- Did they get stuck at any point? If yes, how did they work out of the challenge?

"Why would I care about such detail?" you ask. "The results should be the same."

Yes, the results *should* be the same. But what if they aren't? This is really a communications exercise to determine how clearly one person specified the task(s) and how clearly the other heard them and could translate what they heard into correct action. Micromanagement provides an opportunity to gather additional information about how your partner solves challenges.

It's good news if the result turned out well: you've just had a demonstration that you work well together.

If the experience did not turn out as you'd expected, you'll want to determine the cause of the stumble. Was it from...

- Imprecise directions from the start (you might have glossed over important details or failed to explain the importance of certain sequences);

- Imprecise understanding of those directions (inattentiveness, failure to ask clarifying questions);

- Lack of skills or knowledge to complete the task as you wish (they didn't know that they didn't know how to complete the task, so did not know what questions to ask in the beginning); or whether...

- They messed it up willfully.

By the way, external factors often cause inattentiveness and willfulness. It matters whether either of you are on medications; it matters whether either of you have hormonal imbalances (yes, men too); it matters whether you are under unusual stress, or are ill. It could even matter whether either of you has had a drink before starting a complex task. One drink may be sufficient to blunt your abilities; one drink may make you hypercritical.

Given any of these conditions, it may be hard to tell whether the other is impaired, being inattentive, or is actively resisting a clearly stated preference.

The issue of discerning willfulness from inattentiveness, and what you do about it, is pretty important. The next chapter (on communication theory) is designed to empower both of you to solve these kinds of challenges—ideally, before they escalate.

Some ideas are obvious…

Some ideas are obvious once you hear (or read) them; I've collected a few for you:

- *Communicate:* You can't expect to have what you want if you don't ask for what you want.

- *Create a Joy Jar:* It's a container to hold slips of note-paper. Every day, you each write down an example of how the other person made you joyful that day. When feeling low, pull out and read some of the slips of paper.

- *Complete difficult conversations:* You know it's true: if you don't want to say something, that "something" has to be said and discussed. Communication at this level stabilizes relationships. Closure confers respect. (You've kicked one of the "elephants" out of the room.)

- *Overcome negativity:* You can't create from a negative. Some people react to behaviors of others that they dislike about themselves. Others react negatively to people who are not dressed nicely or are not HWP; advertisers promote these images as "good." It can be hard to overcome such pervasive social conditioning largely because they have become invisible assumptions about who is and is not okay.

- *The last three minutes:* Psychologists have shown that the last three minutes of a conversation or event strongly influence your memory of the encounter. You'll tend to remember that conversation or event as "good" or "bad" based largely on how it ended. By extrapolation, it's VERY important to say loving and supportive things to your partner just as you're going to bed.

Chapter Five
Communication Theory

Most of the time we don't communicate, we just take turns talking.

Anon

Communication is certainly a well discussed topic, with lots of information already written. You might wonder why I would take time to write a book on this subject, considering how well it's already covered.

Answer: This book synthesizes both obvious and often overlooked information from many disciplines—sociology, psychology, business, management, etc.—and delivers the more useful lessons in manageable chunks you can apply to your life.

I'm over seventy. I've been working on my ability to communicate clearly for a long time. Also, because I conduct lectures and workshops on communication, I learn a lot from others. There is a lot of material in this chapter. I provide references for most of the topics so you can do more reading on your own. My purpose is to add communication tools to the skills you have already developed.

The major sections in this chapter are:

- Communication challenges

- Basic skills: speaking and listening

- Nuts and bolts: clarity, reactions, active listening

- Communication effectiveness: simplicity and directness, being in the moment, interpreting inflected speech

- More advanced concepts: transference and projection

A warning (sigh). Parts of this chapter are light (funny), and other parts are dense (thought-provoking). I'll apologize in advance for the denser parts. I'm afraid I don't know a shortcut to presenting this complex material.

#############################

In my experience, communication breakdowns result from a collection of evils. The communications mess usually starts when someone is speaking only from their own viewpoint and hasn't considered the other person's viewpoint. As a result, the speaker sends out messages that are phrased in the speaker's (rather than the listener's) language. Among other things, that means that the speaker has made assumptions about how much the listener knows or remembers about the topic being discussed: also, the speaker is likely to be speaking partly in a private shorthand or code.

Along these lines, communication hick-ups occur when the speaker uses imprecise words, forcing the listener to interpret the speaker's meaning ("You know, like when they sort-of fudge some of the words to avoid, like, telling a secret, right?")

As if this isn't enough, all kinds of distractions can contaminate the overall communication process. For example, even while speaking and listening, both people are simultaneously making judgments about each other, about things going on around them, and about what they're going to have for dinner. This keeps people from being fully present. Bottom line: each party remembers verbal exchanges somewhat differently, and you really need a video of the event to reveal dissimilarities.

This chapter focuses on your own speaking and listening skills. How clearly you speak your message relies on two *listening* skills. The first concerns how correctly your reply matched what was said (how well *you* were listening). The second bears on how well you adapted your own word choices to the other person's listening characteristics. Once we've covered these areas, I'll touch on *transference and projection* before ending up with *upsets*.

Communication Challenges

One person says: "I want XY and Z." The other person says, "Great, I want XY and Z too." How do these people verify that the mean the same "X," the same "Y," and the same "Z?"

Sometimes, it's not so easy: sometimes words are in such common use that you assume you understand them, when you really don't know what the speaker/writer meant.

For example, in my world, the phrase *communication challenges* suffers from the uncomfortable combination of two poorly defined words: **communication** and **challenges**.

Communication describes a process of transmitting an idea between sentient beings. It may involve speaking, using a facial or body gesture, or wearing certain clothing. Right now, I want to use the word to refer to two or more people speaking.

As I've been saying throughout this book, at the most basic level, the way you speak is a result of:

- The situation;

- Your history with those with whom you're speaking;

- Your communication skill level (including your education and work experiences);

- Your emotional state and the emotional states of those around you;

- The intention you have of communicating your message (e.g.: delivering facts, being romantic, managing a crisis);

- Etc.

The way you speak is also influenced at a basic level whether you are speaking:

- *With* someone (two-way communication);

- *At* someone (one-way communication);

- To an audience (lecturing);

- With a brainstorming team (interactive and exploratory; cooperative);

- To a supervisor or to a subordinate;

- Etc.

In English, the word "communication" or "communicating" carries the connotation that the other person is in fact, understanding the messages you are sending. "Communication" is considered to be a back-and-forth process. Statements such as: "I'm communicating with Bill," or "We're in communication," signals the existence of a two-way flow of information.

On the other hand, the word *speaking* carries no such connotation. You could easily be speaking to your neighbor, and in reality, you are simply venting. You're not expecting interaction from the one-way communication.

Challenges can be an equally messy word because of its multiple connotations in English. It can mean:

- Confronted (challenged) by some authority ("Stop! Police!");

- Being confronted with (challenged by) resistance ("I don't want to talk about it.");

- Finding it difficult (challenging) for your hearer to get the message you're trying to send ("I'm sorry, could you please explain that differently?");

- Having to move beyond (challenging) your comfort zone in some way. (For example, being given a particularly difficult academic book to read.);

- So traumatizing (emotionally challenging) to your hearer that he/she shuts down. ("Your stupidity knows no bounds; how could you have possibly thought that I wanted XYZ? Haven't you learned anything about me over the last three months?");

- Etc.

Silly? A stretch? Playing with words? Not really. This kind of silly hair-splitting results from trying to pin specific meanings to mush words, words that mean different things to different people in different situations. Mush words are words that have a subjective rather than objective meaning. Neither "Stop" nor "thief" are mush words; everyone who knows those words also knows how they're meant in general use. On the other hand, while virtually everyone knows generally what "love" means, it *is* a mush word. Here's the "must test" for a word such as "love:" ask some people to define it. You're likely to come up with nine slightly different interpretations/meanings.

Anthony Robbins has commented, "The way we communicate with others and with ourselves ultimately determines the quality of our lives."

This chapter—this book—is not about casual conversation where you may not be paying particular attention to what's going on. ("Hi, how're you doing?" "Great, thanks. I totaled my car yesterday." "Glad to hear it. Take care, now."). Silly example? Well... lately, I've noticed when I enter a store, a salesperson will say, "Hello," but when I say "Hello" back, they answer, "Fine, thanks." Disconnected, are they? Telegraphing a hidden message, are they?

So, the material in this chapter concerns theories, tips, and techniques to help you and your partner become more precise when speaking with one another.

Basic Skills

Speaking

As you've just read, I distinguish between *talking* and *speaking*. One *talks to* someone or *speaks with* someone. In my view, talking is one-way—it's lecturing. By its very nature, lecturing reinforces a knowledge and/or power imbalance and puts the speaker in the dominant role. This distinction is useful both in training (where you may wish to sound as though you know something) and in emotionally loaded discussions (where you're likely to get into trouble).

You can get into trouble *talking to* someone during an emotionally charged exchange because when you sound "authoritative", you also sound *parental.* Those familiar with Transactional Analysis (TA, previously mentioned and to be discussed in depth in Chapter Six) realize that speaking in parent voice can trigger (or sustain) your listener responding in child voice (filled with emotion-laden words). Once you know a bit about TA, you'll learn how to extract yourself from this kind of loop by moving into what is called *adult voice.*

Research and theory confirm that the path to adult conversations involves *speaking with* someone using clear and emotionally-neutral words. Let's tease this apart for a minute. All communication involves the following mix:

- Someone wishes to communicate a message;

- They say something that may or may not communicate that message clearly;

- Even if the speaker actually succeeded in saying the words that carried their intended message, the listener received the message within the context of personal, social, political, and economic filters created from their lifetime of experiences (most strongly influenced by their childhood experiences around which they built life-rules that kept them from emotional or physical pain);

- In an effort to make what was said fit into their universe, the listener interpreted what they *thought* they heard and made it mean something. **The something they made it mean may not be precisely what the speaker meant to communicate.** As Mark Twain said: "The difference between the right word and the almost right word is the difference between lightning and a lightning bug."

Speaking is rather like sex: we think we do it well because we've been doing it all our lives. However, in reality we seldom sit down to study the topic. Unfortunately, when we do something for which we have not been trained, we usually don't do it very well. That's the case for sex and it's the case for communication. Most people experience mediocre sex and imprecise communication.

You might reflect for a minute...

- What evidence do you have that you are able to communicate clearly, confidently, and persuasively? (In your work life, are you looked upon as a particularly clear communicator?)

- Do your ideas have *selling power*? Do other people generally follow your ideas?

- Have you read books or taken courses in effective communication strategies?

- When you speak, do you use simple words, short sentences, and clear word-pictures?

- When your partner describes an experience or a concern, do you take the time to listen actively and then respond in a way that makes the other person feel acknowledged and respected? Does the person with whom you are speaking feel valued and validated?

Listening

It upsets people when they feel they're not being heard. Whether at home or at work, this is one of the most common communication complaints. Fortunately, communication skills (like other skills) improve through practice. In my experience, even realizing that there are different listening levels has helped me to focus and be mindful when listening to others. I pass these on to you in the hopes you find them equally useful.

Listening begins when you are first born with basic sound discrimination. As I mentioned a few pages ago, a baby cries, stops, listens for a reaction, and continues crying. Your listening skills become refined as you develop into adulthood. Some adults have outstanding listening skills; others, not so much. If you'd like to explore this topic, I'd recommend *Crucial Conversations* by Kerry Patterson and Joseph Grenny (previously mentioned.)

While *listening* takes many forms, this list of eight common categories are enough to give you a good overview:

1   Discriminative listening;
2   Comprehension listening;
3   Critical listening;
4   Biased listening;
5   Appreciative listening;
6   Sympathetic listening;
7   Relationship listening; and
8   Therapeutic listening.

Discriminative listening is the most basic type of listening. This is where you learn how to assign meaning to sounds, to interpret voice inflections and emotional nuances. During a conversation, the richness of your understanding depends upon your skills at recognizing and interpreting the speaker's emotional cues.

Discriminative listening is closely allied to discriminative *observation.* It means that when listening, you're trying to pick up shades of meaning; it means that you're trying to interpret the speaker based on what you know about the person. As a resource, I highly recommend a book I've already mentioned: *What Every BODY is Saying: An Ex-FBI Agent's Guide to Speed-Reading People* by Joe Navarro and Marvin Karlins)

Comprehension listening simply means that you're combining your vocabulary, language, and social skills to understand not only the words but also the meaning of what is being said. Of course, the fact that you're reading this book means that you understand someone speaking in your language. However, there can be trouble: comprehension listening can break down under three common conditions:

- The speaker uses imprecise words leaving meanings open to interpretation.

- The speaker uses filler words (e.g.: stuff, things) forcing you to guess what they're talking about.

- The speaker is using coded or indirect speech meant to be understood only by certain people, and that might not include you.

Critical listening enables you to evaluate and judge what is said—as long as the speaker is using clear and direct speech. Critical listening requires more than simply understanding what is being said, it includes the ability to relate what is said to what you know about that topic while simultaneously reading the person's non-verbal cues. (Again, see: *What Every BODY is Saying...*)

Critical listening skills have to be developed. As Peter Drucker said: "The most important thing in communication is hearing what isn't said." To do this, you have to stay present and focused on the speaker.

So, for example, you'll want to overcome the normal tendency to become distracted by self-talk filled with judgments and considerations. You'll want to stay focused even if the speaker misuses a word or says something that you believe is not true. Similarly, you have to avoid getting caught up looking for subtext. Some people don't clearly say what they mean; they use a kind of code or subtext to disguise uncomfortable topics. As a listener, you risk becoming distracted trying to decipher sub-text while simultaneously staying present with the ongoing conversation. That's a skill some do better than others.

Biased listening can occur for many reasons. Commonly, the speaker says something that annoys (triggers) you; your listening is compromised. Your brain reacts by shifting focus from the speaker to yourself. As the speaker keeps talking, you'll only hear part of the message. At this stage, your own stereotypes, insecurities, and assumptions about the speaker or the topic may cause you to further misinterpret what is being said. It is *very common* for a speaker to say "X" and for the listener to hear something wildly different—and then react to what they *thought* they heard. In business settings (and even in some personal settings), the leader is responsible for recognizing when this has happened and to track down the root of the misunderstanding. It's important to take that step if you expect to prevent the same type of misinterpretation in the future.

Appreciative listening occurs when you're in a good mood and listening to something you enjoy. This could be music, poetry or maybe even the tone of your partner's voice. Often, appreciative listening calls forth feelings of gratitude; that's a good thing.

Sympathetic listening is used when we care about the other person and show this concern by paying close attention and expressing sorrow for their ills and happiness at their joys. (By the way, *empathetic listening* requires us to go beyond sympathy to seek a truer understand about how others are feeling. This requires excellent discrimination and close attention to the nuances of emotional signals. When we are being truly empathetic, we actually experience what the speaker is feeling.)

Relationship listening is most common when the bond is new, and each verbal exchange adds to your pool of knowledge of this person. This form of listening also occurs when there is an upset, and you are trying to understand the other person's viewpoint.

Therapeutic listening can be risky if you're not a trained therapist. With some trepidation, I'm going to include it here. Psychologists and trained counselors use *therapeutic listening* to help clients understand, change, or develop in some way. That is, a client brings a problem to the therapist who listens with a "therapeutic ear" and replies in specific ways that encourage the client to explore their issue.

We've been discussing some of the fundamental aspects of speaking and listening. Now, I'm going to move on to suggest ways to help improve communication skills.

Nuts and Bolts

There are ways to engage in an important discussion, and there are ways to engage in an important discussion. This section offers some ideas to help you improve communication in everyday life. I'm going to cover four topics in this section:

- The intent of your questions;
- The clarity of your speech;
- Reacting to something said; and
- Staying present through active listening.

The Intent of Your Questions
It's not only what you say; it's how you say it.

"All true questions are neutral. If a question is not neutral, then it is not really a question, but rather a statement or a judgment disguised as a question. Neutral questions increase intimacy, whereas non-neutral questions create defensiveness and distance. It is not enough for the words to be neutral, the intent of the questioner must also be neutral." So wrote Charles MacInerney in his article, "The Importance of Neutral Questions." I knew this viscerally; I'd never seen it written out. Let's talk about this.

MacInerney gives an example of a child who has done something to upset its mother. Mother reacts strongly saying, in effect: "What in the world made you think you could do that?!" The child becomes defensive and shuts down emotionally. The child recognizes that "upset mother" means that they have done something wrong. They may try to make up answers to Mother's question in hopes of stumbling across one that will placate her. Either way, the way Mom phrased the question shut down communication.

The message: Stay neutral when crafting alternative phrasing. Avoid expressing anger or judgment, just express curiosity. Say, "Why did you do that?"

Neutral questions open the space for the other person to think about what was asked and respond appropriately.

We all tend to make judgments about others in our lives. We have learned our own lessons and (foolishly) made the usual error that other people think (or problem-solve) as we do. I've already mentioned "the usual error," and it's likely to come up again in this book: it's our default mindset, and it keeps tripping us up. In the case of neutral questions, this bias causes us to make judgments about others based upon insufficient evidence. The "loaded question," frequently phrased sarcastically, contains our own judgments. Often these judgments are wrong and hurt our relationships with others.

Again, MacInerney: "Neutral questions present an opportunity to clarify a situation prior to forming an opinion. Other times neutral questions arise from a belief that the other person may well have something more they can share. Neutral questions should never be used as a back handed way to point out a perceived mistake or deficiency."

Here are some key benefits of using neutral questions:

- Neutral questions help slow you down. They help you to become present with the situation and think more deeply before asking a question. (As Jim Hayhurst, Sr. said: "When you don't know what to do, do it slowly.")

- Neutral questions are open-ended. They are intended to encourage the listener to make a thoughtful reply. Thoughtful replies are good; they lead you down the path to meaningful communication.

- Neutral questions avoid revealing a personal agenda. They communicate the speaker's open heart and open-mindedness.

- Neutral questions enable the listener to explain their beliefs or actions without the speaker expressing any pre-drawn suspicions or conclusions. This can provide mutually valuable information, for it enables the speaker and the listener to explore differences or similarities in their beliefs and assumptions about a topic.

However, there are levels of neutrality.

Questions that at first seem unbiased can mask buried agendas, biases, or opinions. It takes practice to develop the skill of asking truly impartial questions. Nevertheless, it's worth the effort (in my opinion) for "you'll find that you're able to look out upon the world with curiosity and a desire to seek the truth, rather than striving to control it."

Neutral questions lead us towards understanding. When a problem is transparent, the solution is easy to see.

Clarity of Your Speech

We all speak: mostly, we think we're understood. The thing of it is, we all speak clearly enough for the level of interaction we're used to. We aren't very sensitive to how much more clearly we *could* speak if we paid greater attention to our own words. Since we're not very aware of how clearly we now speak, we're also not very aware of how "clear and lucid speech" would affect our lives. After all, first impressions are not only comprised of how we dress, stand, and walk. Such things as cultural expectations, accent/dialect, vocabulary, and clarity of speech (to name a few) strongly influence the first impressions we give others.

When speaking informally, particularly with friends, we tend to use imprecise words because the general meaning makes sense. Anyway, our friends sort-of know what we mean. Thus, a sentence: "I have to run. I've got to pick up some stuff before going home" makes perfect sense in an informal setting. Nobody is expecting you actually to run at that moment; nobody is interested in what you have to pick up before getting home.

The quality of your communication has to change to match the importance of the conversation. You can use baby talk with infants; you can't use baby talk with your boss. You can use a fairly informal level of speech with your boss, but not if your Board Chairman is included in the conversation. Speech quality must match the situation when conversations become more socially, politically, or professionally important. At least, that's how it is theoretically. Here are some areas to consider if you wish to raise the quality of your verbal communications:

- Use of filler words (Uh, um, stuff, things, etc.);
- Size of your vocabulary (erudite is better);
- Use of slang and idioms ("Yah, no problem");
- Enunciation (vs. mumbling);
- Pace, tone, and pitch of speech (go for *slow and low*);
- Pre-planning your sentences;
- Breath control;
- Etc.

Words express concepts; your sentences paint pictures. Build your vocabulary; try to rid yourself of mush words. Enjoy the reactions of others as your speech becomes richer.

- "Oh, he brought some stuff over to my house; he wanted me to see his newest toy," gives no information beyond the fact that a man brought something unknowable to a person's house. There's nothing in that sentence that encourages you, the listener, to react.

  "Oh, Jack brought his new 7" Digibig Tablet over to my house last night. It was amazing; it weighed less than a pound. He was really excited to show me the new time-management apps that he's using. I have to admit: I'm going to go out and buy one." Ah, solid information.

- "You make me so sad I'm almost in tears" imparts no information beyond the fact that something unknowable is going on between you and the person you're speaking with, and that something is causing you to interpret their actions with emotional sadness. There's nothing here for you to work with.

  "When you sit next to me looking distracted, I take that to mean that you would rather not be here with me." Ah, solid information.

This sentence construction I used in that last bullet follows a specific pattern meant to open yourself to the other person so they understand the impact of their words. This gives them a chance to clarify what they said or to agree with the way you interpreted what they said. That is a VERY valuable tool. This is the pattern I mentioned about 30 pages ago: *When you (said or did "X") I took that to mean "Y."*

When you use the, "I took that to mean..." construction, you are communicating a clear message to the other person about the impact of their words in your world. This is extremely important when two people are trying to work through any kind of real or perceived emotional hurt.

An alternative to the "...I took that to mean" structure is simply to ask the person speaking to clarify what they just said. Ask: "What did you intend when you said that?" This can be a like a bucket of cold water in a conversation, but it forces both of you to come present and deal with something that has the potential for being misunderstood.

This brings us to the next topic...

Reacting to Something Said

When one person sees another person react to something they just said, the way the initial speaker reacts depends on any number of things:

- The "power" or "authority" difference between the two people;

- The communication and counseling skills of the speaker;

- The speaker's interest in dealing with the other person's reaction;

- Etc.

Apart from those large-scale topics, there are three communication set-ups that can lead to difficulties.

- <u>The topic is one-sided</u>: Only one of you cares about the subject of the discussion: the other person isn't really listening carefully and may miss second-level messages.

- <u>The message triggers something else</u>: On the positive side, the speaker may have triggered memories and the listener has gone off (into their head) to enjoy them. On the negative side, the speaker may have hit a hot button or a landmine and the listener's feelings have been hurt (or the listener has become angry).

- <u>The message sounds like a lecture</u>: One person may *talk to* the other (connotation = lecturing) or *talk at* the other (connotation = responses are unwelcome). Feeling they are being talked down to (diminished, disrespected) they stop listening or build negative feelings about the speaker.

There are polar risks when one person becomes reactive and stops listening. At one end, the ignored speaker may become angry when they realize that the listener didn't seem to understand and/or retain the intended message. Conversely, the speaker may not realize that the other person stopped listening; they assume the message got through. In this second case, the speaker may be doubly angry or upset if a similar situation recurs, because they thought this topic had been thoroughly covered. This is not good; it stresses the relationship.

We've recently discussed the importance of asking neutral questions. Well, there is a technique for avoiding having (or expressing) reactions to things others say to you. The technique is to remain neutral as the listener. The trick to remaining neutral in your responses is *to become aware of what you are about to say before you say it.*

Wherever possible, try to avoid agreeing or disagreeing with people. It sounds radical, I know. However, this mindful practice will train you to control your beliefs and make you aware of your own viewpoints. You'll gain flexibility and a control over your words. Most important, this skill will enable you to control how you express your own beliefs when you don't believe what is being said or done.

- One response to use could be; "that's a good point. Have you considered...?"

- Another possible response is: "I hear what you're saying..."

Finally using active listening techniques will help you to avoid agreeing or disagreeing. Active listening (discussed in the next section) is repeating what the person has said and gaining agreement that you've heard them correctly before you reply.

Oh, and watch your body language. Frequently, we agree or disagree with an unintended nod or shake of our head. Other times may signal our discord by crossing our arms or legs or turning our body toward or away from the person speaking.

Conversations usually occur when someone wants you to agree with them OR is trying to get you to disagree with them so they can defend their position. Listening neutrally disarms the speaker. We generally expect supportive feedback when we speak with someone. If that someone responds neutrally our subconscious mind wonders whether we're on the correct side of the argument (or whether our statement is correct). It can be amusing to watch a speaker as they realize they have lost control over your emotional reactions to what they are saying.

It takes conscious practice to develop this controlled-response skill. It's an act of mindfulness not taught in our culture. We're used to automatically replying to people and this skill requires us to pay close attention to our own replies during normal conversations. It can be a challenge to become an observer of our own words. Observing our own words leads to observing our own thoughts.

As Gary van Warmerdam says in his outstanding online course *Pathway to Happiness,*

> "By keeping your responses *neutral*, you will avoid giving away your own personal power to their position or point of view. You're building your personal power by not wasting it."

van Warmerdam (whose material has strongly influenced this section of the book) points out that people waste their personal power (and burn up their emotional capital) when they judge the world around them by thinking snide or negative comments. Examples include: "Wow, what a stupid driver." "I hate my job." Or "Well, she certainly has no fashion sense!"

When someone makes a statement to you, you can stay in neutral by replying:

- Hmmm, I can't disagree with you.
- Yes, I saw that. It was a surprise, wasn't it?

When you are in the position of being asked to buy or do something and you're being asked questions meant to evoke "yes" answers, you can reply:

- Well, I don't have a firm opinion about that, what do you think?
- That's interesting. What else do you know about it?
- Well, I haven't thought about it before.
- How do you feel about that?
- You've got no argument with me!
- And so forth.

Part of the art of neutral replies is to be so smooth at it that you're not caught. You don't want to appear evasive. For example, if one person is saying something negative about another, you can say...

- I can see how you see them that way.
- You've got no argument from me.
- I don't disagree with you.
- Well, that's very interesting, tell me more about that.

You'll also want to avoid stating (or agreeing with) something that is phrased as a universal truth. If you feel you must make a negative comment, state it as your own opinion. "This rain is horrible; don't you agree?" is phrased as a universal statement prompting another person to agree or disagree. You can get your point across without polarizing the topic. Just state your personal opinion: "I think this rain is horrible."

Now: while remaining in neutral in social interactions is a mindful practice, it's not mindful to do this at work where you're being paid to give an opinion. However, you *can* begin your sentences with some version of: "Well, from my perspective, this is how I see it." Soft openings welcome others to bring up points you might not have considered. However, the power and impact of your words is reduced when you use qualifiers. You'll have to gauge how you want your statements to be perceived.

Conversations in family settings are similar to work settings: you have to state your position in order to provide clear boundaries. You need to communicate your structure and expectations of your family member's behavior.

Here's a subtle but important footnote: in Western culture, we have a social agreement to get along with others. If you're **not** agreeing or disagreeing with someone, they'll notice it. It will affect the stories they make up (and believe) about you.

Staying Present Through Active Listening

If you care about understanding the person speaking with you, you have to put some work into the conversation. You must stay present. Conversations have three elements:

- The words themselves;

- The subtext (hidden meanings) behind the words (that may be discovered by realizing what the speaker is NOT including in the conversation); and

- Non-verbal cues (gestures and mannerisms).

You can usually tell when someone isn't monitoring all these levels because they don't ask the right questions: they're not clarifying and verifying what you're saying. They're *drifting*. They've either grabbed onto something you said and are following that trail, or they've remembered something that's distracted them from the conversation. Either way, their lack of interest will show.

There are some easy and tactful ways of pulling yourself or a "drifting" partner back into the conversation.

- If you realize you're having trouble being present in a conversation and you can't self-correct quickly, you might consider saying something such as: "I'm sorry, but I'm not feeling well right now. Let me get a glass of water; I'll be right back."

- If you sense your listener is not paying attention to you, you might say, "I sense that you have a lot going on right now. Let's stop this conversation for a while and pick it up again at a better time."

There's nothing magical or complicated about these techniques: they're simply suggestions. Obviously, you'll have to reword them to fit your way of speaking.

Now, if you want to go one step further, consider what is called "active listening." Good technique, in my opinion, and very easy to spot. I've always been impressed when someone uses this technique with me. It has the added advantage of being very respectful.

Active listening is the bridge between speaking and listening. This is true for both parties. While I would really encourage you to look it up on the Internet, active listening involves a process that follows a set pattern.

When "Person A" says something, "Person B" restates what "Person A" said and gets "Person A" to agree that "Person B" actually understood what they had said. Only at that point does "Person B" speak a reply to the initial statement. This form of speaking provides three immediate benefits:

- It improves the quality of the conversation: it slows the conversation to give each person time to think.

- It improves understanding that can get muddied during rapid exchanges: the listener has time to realize they may have misheard or misinterpreted something.

- It takes much of the emotional loading out of a conversation: everyone can remain calm.

Here's more of an example: I'll say "ABcD," and the other person says something like, "Let me understand this; you're saying ABcD, is that right?" Wow! I immediately sit up and pay attention; this person is an experienced communicator. If what has been said back to me is accurate, I agree; if the person missed something, I now have the opportunity to clarify. No chance for miscues. As you can see, there is very little chance for the discussion to regress to an emotional level; this communication is referred to as adult-to-adult, in the language of Transactional Analysis, discussed in more depth in the next section.

Respectful processes such as these support relationships of any kind.

I've found active listening to be *extremely* helpful, particularly in potentially stressful discussions. I've most heard this technique used in a business setting where a communication slip can have unfortunate consequences.

There is one last technique to describe before I leave the topic of active listening. Everyone reading this book has experienced it. You ask your partner: "Where do you want to go for dinner?" They reply: "I don't care, where to you want to go?" This goes 'round and 'round for a while. Frustrating. There is a technique to reach a painless decision: ask... "On a 1-10 scale, how much would enjoy eating at 'X'? Okay, on that same 1-10 scale, how about eating at 'Y'?"

This method of quantifying someone's reactions to something resolves quite a bit of communication frustration. You can even use this technique on major or minor issues: "On a 1-10 scale, how much do you want to sell this house?" or "On a 1-10 scale, how interested are you in accepting this job offer?"

You must be clear that there is no punishment for honesty. Your purpose is to help one another reach a balanced decision. Really, you're managing expectations; you're quantifying the other person's needs. This is fact-finding: you're just collecting information so you both have the most successful experience you can.

Ways of Phrasing Things

In a general sense, we're all here on Earth just trying to do the best we can and help others along the way. Our communication styles can make it easier or harder on ourselves and on those around us. As we all know that the way we phrase sentences helps or hinders the message, here are some examples of gentle ways of responding to others:

Asking for more information or verifying your understanding of something:

- "Just to be sure I understand, you would like me to...?"
- "Tell me more about..."
- "So you are saying that... correct?"
- "This is what I understand you are telling me..."

How to take responsibility for answering a question for which you don't know the answer:

- "That is a good question, let me find out for you. You're asking.... is that correct?"

- "I'm not sure, but let me find out for you. Just to be sure I understand, you're asking... is that right?"

- "I'm sorry, I don't have information about that. If you'll give me a few minutes, I'll look it up."

- "I'm sorry, this issue is beyond my expertise. Will you please hold while I find someone who can help you?"

How to say "No" without triggering an upset:
Saying "No" to someone can be off-putting. Depending upon the situation, it may be taken as confrontational and rude. The well-known "Compliment Sandwich" softens the message. John Rydell describes some effective alternatives in his article "Simple Tips on Having the Hard Conversation." Basically, he suggests recognizing the request up-front, then add positive statements that offer a viable compromise to the "no."

- "I'm sorry, we can't afford that trip to Las Vegas, but we could have our own 'lost weekend' at a hotel in town. It's not Vegas, but it's affordable. What do you think?"

- "A movie: what a nice idea. I hate to say this, but that movie is just too violent for me. How about if we work together to make a list of movies we'd both enjoy and pick one of those?"

Making Distinctions

Business executives are paid to make decisions. Often those decisions are based on incomplete information. Successful managers have learned to listen carefully, and to ask questions that help them recognize the information they need to make good choices. However, their path contains some landmines. We're going to tackle two of them in this section:

- The stated issue vs. the real issue; and
- Political expediency vs. tough alternatives.

Stated Issue vs. the Real Issue

Usually, when people say they want to work on issue "X," the issue is "X." Not a problem. What is, is. However, sometimes "X" isn't the real issue; it's only a symptom or an aspect of some deeper underlying issue. You can learn more about the person with whom you're speaking when you sense (or realize) that the topic the other person wants to speak about isn't a core issue. For example:

- The issue they propose to work on may be a more approachable topic than the core concern;

- The issue they wish to discuss may be a "feint," a substitute issue that represents an emotionally safe alternative: the other person is hiding the real issue from you;

- The other person doesn't have the personal insight to realize the topic they've proposed won't resolve their concern/upset;

- Your own blinders and filters cause you to incorrectly assess the importance of the topic the other person wishes to discuss; or

- You assume you understand what the other person wants to speak about because if you were they, *you'd* want to speak about it, too. (This is Jungian projection, previously discussed.)

Here's a common situation: For whatever reason, someone identifies an issue they'd like changed/redefined. It appears visible and thus approachable. It's not hidden, and nothing is clearly connected to it. Well, most things are interconnected, but at this moment, they can't see any interconnectedness. As they get further into discussing the topic, though, they realize that changing this superficial behavior fails to address issues that caused them to notice this item in the first place. They stop working on it for fear of opening up topics that could get away from them; topics they're not prepared to discuss.

For example, if I were to say that I wanted to work on our "welcome home" ceremony, I would really mean that I wanted to work on ways to reconnect emotionally when we've both been at work all day. If we only worked on the ceremony, we'd miss the discussion about what "connection" means for each of us. However, as we start down the "what does connection mean to us" track, we realize that each of us is describing different behaviors that would make us feel "connected." That, in turn, triggers a discussion about what it even means to be "emotionally connected." *That* discussion in turn takes us to: "how do we prefer to spend time together," and *that* also reveals differences.

Now, rather than a simple light-hearted discussion about how we greet one another when coming home from work, we have some very raw core value-differences siting on the table staring at us. Obviously, we realize why our "welcome home" ceremony hadn't been working: it only fulfilled one person's needs—the person who was dissatisfied with it and wanted to discuss it.

This brings up a related topic: building a common lexicon.

As psychology professor Patrick Faircloth mentioned recently in a phone conversation: "If you're going to have a discussion about X, you have to ask the person what THEY think X means. Their reply will help you gauge where each person's beliefs diverge or converge."

This point is really important. If you want to have a discussion about your relationship (for example), it will help if each of you can express out loud what your relationship means to them. What do each of you believe you "relationship" encompasses? Try it out. Have the discussion: each writes down the components, hopes, and expectations of having a partner in a relationship. What are the core relationship rules? Jen had eight; I had five.

At a deeper level, I vividly recall the night my partner and I had our first "word understandings" discussion. It was triggered by her comment that she wanted me to be more "transparent." I asked her what "transparency" meant to her, and how I would behave if I were "more transparent." Wow! New information. She easily described behaviors that (to her) meant I'd be "transparent." However, with Asperger Syndrome, I realized that she was asking for behaviors my brain wiring would fight. I explained that to her. She was not happy.

That's the risk in delving into core values: they may not mesh well.

Sometimes men/women mean something quite specific when they speak; it's just that they are speaking in their own special code. You can begin to suspect this has happened when you've worked through an issue, but your proposed solution seems to be missing the mark. When this happens, you might consider going back to your partner to explore what they thought they said to you. By the way, they'll probably think they were very clear with you: they're so used to their own code they won't understand how you could possibly misunderstand.

Sometimes, what you *think* is the problem simply isn't right.

If you haven't recently read *Men Are from Mars, Women Are from Venus,* by John Gray, 1992, I urge you to revisit it. Although it is a book of "armchair psychology" rather than research work, Gray discusses gender differences and socialization and how these play out in conversations and relationships.

Political Expediency vs. Tough Alternatives

In the context of a relationship, *political expediency* means that one person will do something (or act some way) that is useful or convenient or productive for the relationship rather than for one or the other member of the team.

Political expediency means addressing concerns in ways that don't threaten your relationships' core. Each of you gives a little; each of you learns a new way of speaking together; each of you stakes out off-limit topics. This last point is particularly appropriate when two people begin their relationship: trust is still young. You may not yet trust one another with aspects of their past. For some people, trust is *earned*: for others, trust is *given*.

In that light, this book has been about communication issues. Specifically, it's been about resolvable communication issues. This book has **not** been about solving serious or deep-seated problems that are manifesting through communication problems.

Mitigated Speech

Mitigated speech is a term created by David O'Hare in his 1990 book, *Flightdeck Performance: The Human Factor* and popularized by Malcolm Gladwell in his book, *Outliers.* Mitigated speech is defined as "any attempt to downplay or sugarcoat the meaning of what is being said." Upon close analysis of pilot and copilot conversations recovered from flight recorders after airline crashes, O'Hare made two startling discoveries. First, most crashes occurred when the pilot was in command, not when the copilot was flying the plane. Second, there was a correlation between airline crashes and the cultures from which the copilots were raised. In brief, to the extent that copilots came from cultures with high regard for people with authority, the less likely they were to speak directly about a problem. They found ways of sugar-coating the bad news.

Ultimately, psychologists identified six degrees of mitigation we use when speaking with supervisory staff who have authority over us:

1   *Command:* "Strategy X is going to be implemented."

2   *Team Obligation Statement:* "We need to try strategy X."

3   *Team Suggestion:* "Why don't we try strategy X?"

4   *Query:* "Do you think strategy X would help us in this situation?"

5   *Preference:* "Perhaps we should take a look at one of these Y alternatives."

6   *Hint:* "I wonder if we could run into any roadblocks on our current course."

The way the airline industry has sought to resolve the (often fatal) perils of mitigated speech apply directly to this book on interpersonal communication. Some of us wither and withdraw when someone says something forceful, even when we suspect (or know) it is not correct.

For the airline industry, this problem of pilot/copilot communication was divided into two parts: how to get the copilot to view the pilot as a person like himself (rather than someone with authority over him); second, specific words or phrases the copilot could use to communicate truly seriousness problems (as seen by the copilot).

The first step called for the copilot to use the pilot's first name when using the following speech protocols. The use of the pilot's first name (as opposed to calling him "Captain," per standard protocols) was the first signal that the message that followed the use of the pilot's name was very important for the pilot to understand.

So, let's say that the pilot's name is André. The three phrases available to the copilot are these:

- André, I'm concerned about...
- André, I'm uncomfortable with...
- André, I believe the situation is unsafe

If the pilot has not responded to correct the problem and the copilot continues to believe the aircraft is in immediate peril, he then has the authority to take command of the aircraft.

If you are used to living and working in a strictly egalitarian setting, there can be some challenges translating this system to a work or home situations After all, you're probably used to calling your supervisor, workmates, and domestic partner by their first names. Some readers may be able to signal an important message by going up a step in formality. For example:

- Use Mr., Ms., Mrs., or Dr. either with their first name ("Mr. Bob, I'm concerned about...") Or with their last name, ("Mr. Rubel, I'm concerned about...")

- If you're used to using a "love name" or "pet name" for your partner, you can revert to their legal name (or their full name, as opposed to their nickname). "Robert, I'm concerned about..."

- You are also likely to get their attention by including their first and middle names or their entire names: "Robert Jack, I'm concerned about..." or "Robert Rubel, I'm concerned about..."

  ◦ You knew your parents level of upset by the length of your name they used when first speaking to you after an "incident." If all three, first-middle-last, were used you knew you were in serious trouble.

Clearly, you'll have to discuss this safety alert system and work out a signal that will work for you. You'll also have to practice it a time or two in order to connect the idea that the unusual way of addressing your partner is part of a signaling system that something is going wrong and requires their focused attention.

Consider the possibility that some of your communications challenges have resulted from your desire to respect authority. Most of us are taught to respect authority, and such respect has its place. However, "showing respect" doesn't mean you are to permit someone you feel has more authority (or more experience or seniority) than you to misinterpret what you are saying or make a mistake that would affect an important outcome.

Now that you know about mitigated speech, you are the person with specialized knowledge. There's no advantage in having specialized knowledge or skills unless you use them.

Venting: be a Good Listener

In my experience, "venting" is gender-linked: sometimes, the woman just wants to talk. Sometimes, she needs to unload emotionally about something that happened that day. Men, helpful things that we are, want to be "helpful" and offer "suggestions." Don't do that. If you engage in the dialog, you're likely to become drawn in to the drama. Just listen. Your approved responses are:

- Wow!
- I could see how that would upset you.
- People can certainly surprise you, can't they?
- It baffles me how someone could do that.
- I see.
- You handled that very well.
- Well, tomorrow's a new day.
- And so forth.

Often, women wish to relate an experience just to get it out of their systems. The very *last* thing they want is someone to tell them what they *should have done* or what they *should do tomorrow* to fix it. They're not interested in hearing your ideas about fixing it. They're plenty smart, and they understand their work politics: if *they* don't know how to fix it, YOU certainly don't. Worse, unless you're pretty sophisticated in listening for word prompts that signal emotional states, you risk replying in *parent voice* (making parental-like pronouncements and offering solutions) rather than reply in *adult voice* (that is neutral and free of emotions). Replying with *coulds* and *shoulds* (in an authoritative, parent voice) will likely trigger a negative emotional reaction on top of the venting. That's the polite way of saying that you'll make matters much worse and may well cause the person with whom you're speaking to drop into *child voice* (filled with emotional statements) and focus on what an ass you are. My advice: beware, for you're about to have an emotional meltdown. If you're curious about ways that word choice can help or hurt your more serious relationship discussions, you can look up *Transactional Analysis*. (We'll discuss/describe TA (as it's called) in a few pages in the section titled: "Speaking from Your Ego State".)

Improper listening is as damaging as improper speaking. They are equal sides of the communications equation. So: what can you do? You can become a better listener.

"How can you practice *good listening habits?" you ask.* Here are some suggestions:

Give Full Attention

The first habit of listening is to pay attention to the person who is speaking. Give them your full attention—and visibly so. Attend not only with your ears but with your whole body. Turn to face them. Gaze intently at them. The trick to *full attention* is to do it from inside your head, not just by moving your body. If you can be truly interested (which is often just a matter of attitude) then your body will happily follow your mind.

Help Them to Speak

Sometimes the speaker has difficulty getting their points across. Maybe they are not very good at speaking, or are seeking to explain a complex concept. You can help them and yourself by practical encouragement. One good approach is to ask positive questions, both to test your own understanding and also to demonstrate interest.

Show your consideration of the other person through your actions. Help the person to feel good about themselves.

Remember: the person listening to you has a distinct value set and has had a world of life-experiences you don't know about. They may bring a different (and useful) perspective to the discussion. They may know things about what you are saying that you don't know. If you find that you disagree with them, it's prudent to differ with what they are saying rather than with the *person*. Show your acceptance of their right to differ with you while stating your opposition to what they say.

These brief discussions of speaking and listening skills plays into our next section about transference and projection.

Communication Effectiveness

Good relationships are built on clear communication. Obviously, but it's impossible to do this well all the time. You may wish to set up some signals (rules?) when you wish to have certain kinds of communication. For example:

- I'm going to vent now. Don't give me advice.

- I'm sharing an emotional experience. I need some empathy, here.

- I'm angry at what you've just done and you'd better pay attention to how you handle the next ten minutes.

- You've just broken your word: we had agreed to X and you've just done Y.

- We're just chatting: we're just enjoying one another. Nothing heavy going on.

- I need quiet time. Don't speak to me.

- Etc.

Here are some of my pet topics to get you started thinking about communication effectiveness.

We've all had the experience that we think we've understood something really well only to discover that we completely mis-understood what the person meant to say. We're never quite sure whether we misheard or they were not clear. Here are some tips to help in three areas:

- Simplicity and directness;
- Being *in-the-moment* when Speaking; and
- Interpreting inflected speech.

Simplicity and Directness

"Ah, just bring that stuff in here. Oh, and would you please run to my toolbox and bring me my needle-nosed pliers and the small dikes? Oh, and my mallet."

- Stuff?

- Needle-nosed pliers?

- Dikes, he has dikes in his tool chest? (For us old guys, "dikes" are short for "diagonal cutters.")

- Mallet?

How about: "As you're going to the grocery store, would you mind picking up a steak for dinner?"

Steak? Would that be lamb, veal, pork, beef? How thick? What quality? How much? Cost range?

Frankly, I hadn't thought of asking any of those questions, or we wouldn't have had our "Oops" moment. When our relationship was fairly new, I'd volunteered to go grocery shopping. Following directions, I brought back a steak: a sirloin tip steak. Looked fine to me. It fit the direction that I'd been given: "Pick up a steak for dinner."

Well... that's not the kind of steak *she* had in mind for our dinner. She explained (delicately, after her initial surprise) that a steak like this has no marbling and is tough as nails and is used for roasting, not grilling! We laughed about it later, but when it happened, it caused a "hiccup" in that evening. Actually, I went back out to the store for a different steak.

This brings us back to simplicity and directness in speech. When you speak, do you use simple words, short sentences, and clear word-pictures? Check out this example, slightly modified from its source: Charles Stewart University, Division of Student Services, English Support, *Style*:

> **Original sentence:** Research into the life expectancy of the variety of domesticated animals of the species *Sus*, commonly referred to as pigs, has shown that the greatest threat to the possible decline of this species has been engendered by the predatorily inclined *Canis lupus*, often called wolf, and its preferred diet of small mammals.

> **First revision:** Research has shown that predatory wolves threaten the population of pigs, especially those of the small variety.

> **Final result.** Farmers beware: wolves eat small pigs.

Conclusion: "Keep it simple, stupid." Use as few words as you can; it keeps the communication clear. It's easier to understand short sentences not spoken in vernacular. Don't obfuscate through opaque syntax and esoteric vocabulary. Don't be sententious. (He's making a point by being playful.).

Be "In the Moment"

Being "in the moment" can be difficult to explain. Let me do it this way. When something is done, it's over. Once it's over, you go on to the next thing. There is an intersection between "over" and "next." That's where you live when you are "living in the moment."

This situation applies to any people who are speaking. The question is: Is the listener truly *present* for the conversation? Are they listening with intent, or only *pretending* to be listening, letting their mind drift elsewhere? When someone speaks for no discernable purpose, the other person realizes the fluffiness and may tune out. They're not really *hearing* you. Think about your evening conversations. You've both arrived home from work, and you're telling one another about your days. Is the other person *really* listening? After all, your story is basically the same day-after-day. No personal insights; no fresh adventures; no new ideas. Your partner may wonder why you are speaking.

I bring this up if one or the other of you is using casual social conversation to describe situations containing emotional undercurrents and subtexts. Please consider, it's quite possible that your listener is missing it. Unless the listener can recognize differences between this chatter and important discussions, the speaker is likely to feel that they've been given some time off from thinking: their job is just to sit and listen. This is not good for your relationship. The two of you may want to work out signals that mean, essentially, "Pay attention to me: I need to speak about this."

Now, let's turn the tables around. Rather than being the speaker, you're now the listener. The new question is: "How are you communicating your attentiveness? If sitting, are you sitting forward, letting your body language communicate attentiveness? Are you maintaining eye contact? Are your replies supporting the conversation? Are you repeating what you thought you heard (active listening)?"

There are many reasons such in-the-moment presence can be hard for a person. One challenge is to develop the skill to quiet your own background noise and listen to the speaker with focus. You can practice this by listening to the news on the radio. See how long you can listen to the broadcast without your mind refocusing to some personal thoughts. You'll be surprised how difficult this can be.

In face-to-face (or even telephone) conversations, such attentiveness shows honor and respect towards the speaker—always a good thing.

Interpreting Inflected Speech
Oh, this one is fun! You can get into so much trouble, here.

English is typically considered to be what is called an end-stopped language. That is, meaning is carried through the words themselves; changing the tone or pitch of a word does not change *the basic meaning* of the word, as it does in an inflected language such as Chinese. That is, one word in Chinese may have widely unrelated meanings depending upon how it's inflected and the context of the sentence. In English, one word, such as "rock" can't become "atom" with another pronunciation and then "horse" with another.

Notwithstanding this difference between an end-stopped and inflected language, in English, a *huge* amount of the sense and connotation (spin) of a word or sentence depends upon the inflection you give to it. (By the way, this is why it's so hard to teach English to native foreign speakers.) Now, this is difficult for me to do in writing, but try this:

1   "Please close the door." Spoken evenly. No inflection. This is the inflection you would expect when going into a business meeting with someone of higher rank who asks you to close the door. (First request. Simple request. No inflection, but because of that, not particularly friendly.)

2   "PLEASE close the doOR." Said with a smile, the "please" is pitched higher than the rest of the sentence, but you come up a little bit at the end of "door." (Gentle request, very inviting.)

3   "PLEase close the door." The "please" starts high and trails off; the rest of the sentence is said quietly and with expiration. (Said to someone who repeatedly fails to close the door and needs constant reminders.)

4   **"PLEASE** close the door." (You've asked before and were ignored. You're getting testy.)

5   "Please **CLOSE** the door." Said with feeling. (Don't just leave it ajar, you idiot; any fool should know to **close** it for this kind private meeting.)

6   "Please close the **DOOR.**" (Evidently there was some confusion about what you wanted closed and they closed the wrong thing or there was an obvious choice between "door" and something else.)

7   **"Puh-LEE-ze** close the **DOOR."** (You've made this re-
     quest to this person repeatedly and they seem not to
     remember your request. You're exasperated.)

8   "Please **CLOSE** the **DOOR."** —Said shortly and curtly.
     Expresses anger at a request ignored.)

Now, in everyday speech, try this:

1   ok—both letters pronounced the same and at about the
     pace you would say the alphabet. (Everything is fine, I
     understand, no problem.)

2   OooooohkaY—voice falling on the Ooh part and rising
     on the Kay part. (I'll go along with it, but I don't really
     believe you.) NOTE: The longer you draw out the "oooh"
     phase, the more you communicate resistance to the idea
     that you're agreeing to because you feel you have no
     choice in the matter.

3   oohKAy—voice rises to crest at KA and falls suddenly. (Got
     it. I don't necessarily agree with it, but YOU'RE the boss.
     I'm paid to follow directions. I understand your decision.)

4   ohKaaay—Oh is pitched lower than the Kaay. (Time's up,
     that's it, let's go.)

5   Ohkay—Oh starts out as the highest pitch and the pitch
     drops steadily. (Alright, I've had enough of this bullshit.
     Now here's what we're going to do.)

6   OhKAY—short "oh" strong "KAY". (You've got a deal!
     This is it. Just fine. No problem).

7   OhKAY?—short "oh" and "KAY" is upward inflected to
     end as question. (If speaker is smiling, is said in order

to confirm whether or not the listener is on board with the idea. If accompanied with a slight twitch of the head, would mean: "By the way, this is the way I want this done, do you have a problem with that?)

8   kaY?—upward inflected. (Is this OK? Subordinate is speaking to someone of higher authority. Speaker may not be quite sure if it is, in fact, ok to proceed.)

9   I'll stop, here, but I think you can come up with a few variations and interpretations on your own.

This is why communicating through email so often can be misinterpreted. Clearly, it's not just *what* you say; it's *how* you say it.

Transference, Projection, and Trust

Speaking and listening are tremendously affected by transference and projection. Speaking personally, I think that these issues have given me more trouble over the years than any other aspect of communication.

In psychology, *transference* refers to the unconscious process of redirecting feelings about one person to another person. For instance, you might mistrust somebody who shares some of an ex-partner's manners, voice, or physical looks. Or, you may feel submissive to someone who resembles one of your parents or someone you have viewed as an authority figure.

Psychological *projection* (or projection bias) is the term used to describe an ego defense mechanism wherein you attribute (or *project*) your own unacceptable or unwanted thoughts or/ and emotions to another person. This occurs because you're sensitive to (dislike) some aspect of your own behavior and when you see someone else exhibiting somewhat similar behavior, you may react negatively to that person even though this other person hasn't yet done anything to demonstrate unworthiness or distrust.)

For example, projection occurs when Person A projects his/her own interpretation of an act onto Person B and then reacts to Person B *as if* they had reacted as Person A imagined they did. This situation can occur when one person is not listening carefully to another, when one person is guilty about something and is trying to shift the blame, or when a person projects personal insecurities or weaknesses onto the other partner and then reacts to those projections.

Worse, the person being blamed is not at fault. Either there has been some serious breach of trust perceived by the person doing the blaming or the person doing the blaming is personally insecure about something and is lashing out.

- If the projection concerns a perceived breach of trust of your partner, you probably have a communications challenge.

- If the projection is not specific and occurs rather randomly, it may well result from low self-esteem. In that case, the one doing the projecting is likely to have a lot of personal work to do.

It doesn't take a rocket scientist to realize that once one person starts reacting to their own projected insecurities, the relationship has headed down a path filled with misunderstandings, hurt feelings, and mutual bitterness.

If one partner's projections go unchecked, both partners will increasingly grow wary of one another. One partner is seeing dragons under the bed while the other partner can't figure out what they did to trigger this negative pattern.

The highest cliff you can fall from is trust.

"Collapse" and Mark Twain
Something happens.

Immediately, we assign meaning to this event, categorize its importance, and draw conclusions. Usually, we decide upon an action, sometimes defensive, sometimes aggressive. We form lingering opinions.

This collapse between what happened—and the meanings we assign—takes place so quickly that we aren't aware that "what happened" and "what we took that to mean" are two independent and totally separate occurrences.

One reinforces the other and a vicious circle is set in motion.

In that collapse, realities unwittingly get set. Your feelings are hurt. You won't talk about it. In most cases, you assume you took away the correct understanding of the triggering event, so you don't feel there is any need to discuss it further.

That's where Mark Twain comes in: "It's not what you don't know that gets you in trouble. It's what you know for sure that just ain't so."

Chapter Six
Communication Styles

The thing about successful communication is that it's complicated. It's complicated by your age, gender, background, and life experiences. It's complicated when one person knows quite a bit more than the other about communication. It's complicated when one person feels that the other person is constantly hitting them with micro-assaults, micro-aggression. Hurt people hurt people, as I've already said.

This section is intended to expose you to some ways of thinking about communication. You may be familiar with some of these; others may surprise you.

- Information processing modalities
- Love languages
- Speaking from your ego state
- Importance of words

Information Processing Modalities

I've given many situations where people run into communication breakdowns because they don't get the message the way the sender meant it. Now, I'll discuss communication challenges that arise when the sender uses sense-related words that don't resonate with the receiver. Let me explain.

As humans, we must depend upon our five senses to give us a composite picture of reality. There are no alternatives; we have no way beyond our five sensory channels of evaluating the physical world. Our interpretation of our world becomes our reality. Our reality, then, is a combination of what our eyes see, what our ears hear, what our touch feels, and how we feel internally. To a lesser extent, it is also what our tongue tastes and what our nose smells.

Blended together, these senses create our unique frame of reality; no one really experiences it the same way we do. Over time—from your infancy to adulthood—you've come to rely mostly on one or two of these senses. You may be okay reading (visual) but you're better at listening (auditory). While we never stop using our other senses, we gradually develop a preference for one of them.

Translated into your daily life, if you're highly visual, you probably like your possessions to look a certain way in your home; the neatness of your home may matter more than its cleanliness. You may like to dress up or make yourself physically attractive to others, signaling your preference for a visual friend/partner.

If you are highly visual, you may also:

- Remember what you see more easily than what you hear;
- Remember the world in pictures; and
- Prefer to read difficult material rather than to listen to it.

If you don't process visually, then you are likely to be far less concerned about visual issues. This is relevant for communication, because communication effectiveness depends upon building rapport, and to build rapport, you're going to need to know how to determine not only how *you* take in information, but also how others take in information.

Since lack of rapport can doom a relationship of any kind, the more you know about identifying and mirroring other people's reality-processing preferences the easier it will be to communicate with them. For example, if a high-visual person gives a gift of flowers to a high-kinesthetic person without hugging them or touching them, the gift may not be received as the giver had intended. Similarly, if someone who is highly kinesthetic reaches out to touch your arm and you don't respond with a broad smile and a reciprocal touch, the person offering the connection may feel hurt or rejected.

Mismatches such as these can be problems in search of solutions.

Here's a quick review of the five principal ways people take in information from the world around them. As you see, they reflect the five senses and represent some of the different ways you may wish to adjust your own normal preferences to meet your hearer's preferences—in order to help the other person better understand what you're talking about.

Auditory: Listen closely to how your partner phrases ideas, thoughts and feelings, in order to learn how best to respond with matching phrases. Any mismatch in speaking styles is likely to set off alarm bells that your partner may not be able to name, but make them feel slightly uncomfortable. This person will use words such as; "I hear what you're saying," "That sounds good to me," or "I hear you".

Visual: How you look, how your home looks, and how each of you dress can be very important. Particularly early in your relationship, you each want to remove as much outside relationship-clutter as you can, and mismatches in the areas mentioned here are likely to make one or both of you uncomfortable—probably at the subconscious level. The visual speaker uses words such as; "I can see what you're saying." "I see what you mean." "I can see where you're going with this."

Kinesthetic: Does your partner touch you? Does your partner specifically *not* touch you? How and where you touch her becomes another indication of how each of you prefers to take in information. If one of you is strongly kinesthetic and one is strongly something else, you guys need to work this out. I know a couple where the woman would come up to her husband when he was working at his desk or reading a book, and touch him to communicate her love. The problem was, her husband was high visual and not at all kinesthetic. He told me that until he learned about these concepts, he would get furious at having his concentration interrupted—and would stay upset for some time. By the way, if this describes you, you might consider working out an action that won't trigger a negative reaction. One alternative would be to create an action that has your partner standing in the doorway until recognized. This way, it's easy to disengage from work at your own pace and greet your partner with a smile on your lips. If you need more touch than your partner, you may be able to work out either a protocol or a ritual to get that need met.

The kinesthetic speaker uses words such as; "That feels right to me". "I'm comfortable with that". "I'm touched by that story"

.

Gustatory: For some people, the celebration of life translates into wanting to prepare complicated and sophisticated meals. This happens to be my own personal preference. If this is also your preference, then you may wish either to seek out a partner who is a gourmet cook, or send your partner to cooking school. Also, you'll want to recognize each meal as an *I love you* event and respond in kind. Gustatory people use phrases such as: "Ooh, You're so good I could just eat you up!"

Olfactory: One (or both) of you may care a great deal about how the other person smells. If your partner processes by smell, the greatest tip-off is that he or she probably sniffed your neck early in your relationship. You evidently passed that test, but now your cologne selection becomes an issue, as does any decision to use incense or scented candles in your home. These people use words such as; "That doesn't smell quite right to me". When you hear this, you'll have to quickly readjust your vocabulary (and discussion topics) to mirror this person's information processing preferences.

Here are examples of charts designed to help the person of the other gender get on the same page with you. Notice that the charts are filled out as if the person were alone to do as they pleased. This is important, because in relationships, one partner will often alter their behavior to please the other person. The stress of not getting needs met at the sensory level can have a long-term adverse effect on the relationship.

Remember: these charts are totally made up. For example, the woman in the first profile has no particular preferences for visual stimulation or smell. The chart for the man shows very little tolerance for sound or for touch. For the two of them to make a life together, they're going to have to work through these differences.

From the woman's perspective

	Auditory	Visual	Kinesthetic	Gustatory	Olfactory
When I concentrate or work	Techno music		Tapping to the beat	Eating chips or salty foods	
When I relax	Sing		My rocking chair	Sipping iced tea	
When I'm having an upset	Sing with my country music		Go for a drive	Eat a bag of chocolate chips	

From the man's perspective

	Auditory	Visual	Kinesthetic	Gustatory	Olfactory
When I concentrate or work	Silence	Everything has to be in order		Drink ice water	Burn leather incense
When I relax	Silence	See beautiful things all around me		Drink hot black coffee	Smoke a cigar
When I'm having an upset	Silence	Nothing looks right		Drink a stiff Scotch	

If you wish to better understand sorting parameters and their impact on communication, my favorite book is: *Instant Rapport* by Michael Brooks, 1990.

The bottom line is that to have the best effect on being heard and understood by someone else, you will want to present information according to **their** preferred processing style. This is true whether it's a personal or professional relationship. You can learn how to identify their information-processing style by listening to their language (I *hear* what you say; I *see* what you mean; I *know* what you mean; I *feel* your pain; I *sense* that...).

Love Languages

Once you start to listen for the meanings of words your partner is using to speak with you, and once you start listening for the meaning words you are using with your partner, it's better than even money your communication will improve rapidly.

This leads to how you can say *I love you* in a way that your partner can understand. In his book (*The Five Love Languages: How to Express Heartfelt Commitment to Your Mate),* Gary D. Chapman lists five most common ways people can communicate love. It's a good resource. Chapman explains why a loving relationship can founder and how to recognize and appreciate acts of love, even if they aren't something you would normally associate with the concept of love. The overall conclusion is that it's important to know how you want love expressed to you and it's important that your partner knows about their own language of love. Obviously, this topic is worth a good sit-down discussion.

Often referenced, these are Chapman's general observations:

Money/gifts: Some people (usually men) feel that turning their paychecks over to their spouse is their demonstration of love and commitment; they don't have to do or say much (or anything) more. The money is the complete statement of love. For others, gift-giving has a deep meaning, a signal that you know exactly how to please your partner and can demonstrate it through gifts. For people who interpret gifts as love-statements, a single chocolate truffle can mean more than repeatedly hearing *I love you.*

Physical touch: Some people thrive on being touched. When they drive together in the car, one person may be stroking the hand or arm of the other. High-kinesthetics (as they are called) would interpret back rubs or foot massages as *I love you* statements. For them, even brief hugs can be reaffirming.

Performing services: Some people translate; "I'm keeping the house neat" or "I run all your errands for you" as *I love you* messages. They may demonstrate an act of service rather than speaking the words. For example, if one partner is outside the house in a rainstorm trying to fix something, the other partner (who performs service as a love gesture) may bundle up and go outside to help the other person.

Let me expand on the topic of "performing services." Some people avoid emotional connection with the issue or situation by performing service. Rather than have a serious discussion, rather than to express hurt, they perform a service as though nothing was wrong. They are inserting "routine behavior" for "you've just hurt my feelings." Sometimes their partner figures this out; often it goes unnoticed. Here are some ideas if you suspect that your partner is performing service to avoid engaging in uncomfortable discussions. Oh: if you use any of the following "sentence strings," you are ethically required to set up ground rules that state that none of what is revealed can be used against them.

- Tell me what you're happy about in our life... what are your hopes?

- How can our interactions be changed to support your hopes?

- What are our sticking points/stumbles?

- If you had a magic wand that would change some of my behaviors, what would you change?

Time and attention: Some people consider that spending a lot of time with them translates to a love statement. For example, for some, the amount of time that you will spend with them is an indicator of the depth of your love. In answer to the question, "Do you love me?" such a person might say, "Of course I love you; I'm here, aren't I?"

Verbal: Some people respond primarily to being told they are loved. This can also include thanking someone for their help or attentiveness, and also verbal rituals of affirmation ("good job," "nice work," "I really appreciate it when you...").

Obviously, it's important that both partners feel accepted for the language of love they bring to the relationship, and also that they are able genuinely to accept their partner's language of love. The thing of it is, not everybody knows these love languages and there are a lot of missed opportunities within couples when one person's love message goes unrecognized by the other person. If there are too many of these missed opportunities, one partner may grow to feel unloved. This is seldom a deliberate act; it's an invisibility issue. "Let's go out for dinner" may really mean, "Tell me you love me."

Let's explore this path for a sec. Miscues can look like this:

- It's the end of a long workday. She wants a foot rub. Remembering how the house looked with fresh flowers, he's brought some home. She doesn't get it, and you don't get that she doesn't get it. Result: the evening is just a little subdued. She's conflicted, because you were really sweet to bring home the flowers, but now a request to rub her feet may seem excessive, so she doesn't ask. Her needs aren't fulfilled, she doesn't really like flowers (that she had to put into a vase) and you're clueless.

- You want to come home to a nice, romantic meal, and she wants to get out of the house and go to a restaurant. In this case, *getting out of the house and going to a restaurant* may actually contain a new miscue. If she's thinking (but not telling you) that she's meaning a restaurant with linen service and subdued lighting, but you take her to a fast-food joint, you've invited more trouble to join you at dinner.

The possibilities for missing the mark are endless; the possibilities of success are spectacular. Once you are both aware of the different languages of love, you can begin to spot and acknowledge acts of love in the other, even if they don't meet your particular needs. As you can imagine, it becomes important to explore with your partner how he/she feels love.

It's wonderful when both have the same language of love, because it is easy to see and appreciate the other's efforts. However, when the language of love is different, it means that both partners will need to:

- Acknowledge the other's expressions of love even if it isn't particularly meaningful to you,

- Attempt to communicate love in the language that is more easily understood and appreciated by your partner, and

- Discuss individual preferences with your partner so that the other person will know what you want. Don't make them guess and then find fault with them for not guessing correctly.

If you wish to explore this topic in more depth, take a look at some of the NLP (Neuro-Linguistic Programming) material that is available. This is a field unto itself and a course of study that I highly recommend. This will bring you very rewarding personal skills that will affect your work life as much as it does your relationships.

There is a topic closely related to love languages that comes up every so often between genders particularly when tasks or emotional topics are involved. At its core, the issue seems to be the way men and women in the US are brought up.

Earlier I mentioned John Gray's book *Men Are from Mars, Women Are from Venus.* That's a book all about gender-linked misunderstandings.

Now, realizing that either you or your partner may be an exception, the different ways men and women are socialized in Western cultures also affects some very basic preferences.

In the opening chapter, Gray points out that in a general sense, men are brought up to be more interested in *objects* than with feelings or emotions, while women are just about the opposite. He notes that in a general way, women are taught by our culture to fantasize about romance while men are taught to express power by creating results and achieving their goals.

Some of these differences may creep into your dynamic because:

- When the guy asks his partner to help with an object-oriented task, he may be playing into the woman's weak area.

- When the lady seeks conversation and intimate time with the guy, she may be playing into the male's weak area.

I'll leave this section with a suggestion—develop selective blindness. Learn to overlook certain behaviors/characteristics. Learn to communicate in all the languages of love, and learn to recognize and to value the ways others convey their love for you. Oh, and be sensitive to your partner's areas of strength and weakness. Play to strength, it builds your relationship.

Speaking from Your Ego State

Are you on the same page when you try to work through a conflict? Transactional Analysis (TA) may help explain why your best communication intentions can suddenly take an unintended turn—often, to your surprise.

All quoted material in this section comes from the writings of Alan Chapman (www.businessballs.com/transact.htm).

According to Chapman, Eric Berne formulated the concept of Transactional Analysis (TA) in the 1950s. He had observed that personal relationships almost always involve one person speaking with another person; TA is focused on understanding how and why verbal communications between two people succeed or fail. (TA won't apply for Internet or IM communications, because word inflection carries meaning in spoken English, and you need to be able to interpret word inflection to perform this analysis.)

TA is important for our discussion of communication within the relationship, because, as you will soon see, successful verbal interchanges are much more difficult to attain when volatile emotions are involved. As the saying goes, the dice are loaded against you.

Berne was able to pinpoint three **alter-ego states** that exist to one degree or another in every person:

- Parent ego state
- Adult ego state
- Child ego state

All three ego states combine to make up a whole person's personality. Succinctly:

- Your *parent voice* projects what you've been **taught** to understand life to be.

- Your *adult voice* projects the **thoughts** that form your conception about life on earth (it's what you say when you speak to yourself).

- Your *child voice* projects your conception of life in terms of **emotions** (feelings).

Parent Ego State: The *parent voice* is that of "authority, absorbed conditioning, (and) learning and attitudes from when we were young." To some degree or another our own parents, close relatives, friends, and teachers have influenced each of us. For most of us, though, it was our parents who implanted within us the greatest number of often-hidden, as well as clearly overt, ideas that now make up who and what we are. Berne proposed that many of our verbalized ideas often start with certain phrases that are, in fact, learned attitudes. For example, I've heard people soften their comments by starting a phrase with:

- "It seems to me I've read somewhere..."
- "You might consider..."
- "That's a good point; have you thought about..."

Our *parent* perspective on life is formed by external events that have influenced us as we grew up. Although it's often quite difficult, we actually can change our present-day reactions to triggers that set off our pre-programmed responses. For example, if your parents went through the Great Depression of the 1930s and lived frugally for the rest of their lives, you may find it very difficult to spend money on frivolities that you can easily afford, even to this day.

Child Ego State: The *child* state represents the way we react (through feelings) to events outside our life. This part of us embodies our visual (seeing), auditory (hearing), kinesthetic (touching), and the emotional (feeling) makeup. When we seem overcome with feelings such as anger or despair, and the reaction is so much more intense than would normally be expected, it's a signal that our inner *child* is has taken over.

As with the *parent voice,* we can change our reactions, but not easily. For example, if your parents used to call you lazy or messy, you are likely to have to retrain yourself to neutralize your emotional reactions to those words (emotional landmines, in our language).

***Adult* Ego State:** Our *adult* persona represents our capability to think and to act for ourselves, based on our abilities to correctly decode/interpret what is being said to us. Children, even under a year old, begin to learn the lessons that will ultimately form their *adult* ego state. If we are to change our *parent* or *child* ego states, we must do so through our *adult* ego state.

You may wonder why I'm going into this level of detail about Transaction Analysis. The answer is that in my opinion, it is particularly relevant when you run into an upset in the context of a relationship. We all communicate from one or another of our own ego states—our *parent, adult* or *child* states. The situation —and our own frame of mind—determines which persona will do the talking. Moreover, something can trigger a shift from one state to another and back again, without missing a beat.

Berne's great discovery was that communications between people must be **complementary** in order to be successful. That means that for the communication to work, the response should be from the same ego state as the initial communication. If one partner begins the exchange from the *child* ego state, the response must also be from the *child* ego state, or the transaction is said to be *crossed*. This often triggers a communications breakdown. The simplest result of a crossed communication could be that the real message simply falls flat; neither of you quite understands what the other person missed, so you're both sort-of equally confused.

In the ideal communication model both parties speak in the adult ego state. If you find yourself facing a statement from someone that is coming from their *parent* or *child* ego state, you may be able to move the conversation away from the land of emotions or judgment and back to stability by replying from your *adult* ego state.

NOTE: If you're primary goal is to *defuse* the situation, respond from the same ego state that the person used to address you in the first place. However, if your intent is to *resolve* the issue, you should reply in the *adult* ego state and try to encourage the other person to keep the dialog at the *adult-to-adult* level.

A quick example of such an exchange...

"Person A" delivers what is supposed to be a levelheaded non-emotional message from the *adult* ego state. Unfortunately, what they said triggered an emotional reaction from "Person B" who (now upset) replies from a *child* ego state ("You don't even care what I feel!" "What do you even know about it?").

The path to a solution lies first in realizing what has just happened (crossed communication) and then to use skill and tact to bring Person B to the point they can discuss this upset from their *adult* ego state.

Okay, that example was purely theoretical; let's try to make it more real.

Domestic example:

- Him—making a statement from *adult* ego state: "How's our project coming? Are you going to be able to finish your part of it tonight?"

- Her—reacting in *child* ego state: "Wow! I forgot all about it. TONIGHT! No way! I've been working all day. I don't have enough energy to work much more on it."

- Him—responding in *parent* voice: "Now just a minute, honey! If I'm going to do 'X' tomorrow, you know you have to finish 'Y' tonight."

- Her—still in *child* ego state: "I can't stand it when you speak to me that way. If I have to stay up and finish this, then I'm going out with the girls tomorrow night."

- Him—still in *parent* voice: "Perhaps. That depends how well you finish project, since it affects how much more work I can do with our project tomorrow."

- Etc.

As this last reply is another crossed communication. Although this exchange started with a neutral adult-voice question, when she reacted from her *child* ego-state, he triggered an emotional response by replying from his *parent* ego state. Once he did this, they became locked in a parent-child emotion-filled exchange. At the end of this short exchange, she suspects that he's missed her underlying message, which is that she's burned out.

The exchange would have proceeded more smoothly if his reaction to her initial response had also been in *child* (rather than *parent*) ego-state. For example, he could have countered with: "Jeez, what can I say? We really need this completed. Anyway, without your help, I won't get any free time, either. Hey, want to go out for an ice cream cone when we get done?"

To complicate matters a bit more, look at these statistics. Chapman cites Albert Mehrabian (Professor Emeritus of Psychology, UCLA.) for these:

- Only 7% of meaning is transmitted in the actual spoken words.

- 38% of meaning is derived from the way that the words are spoken (emphasis, inflection, connotation, etc.).

- 55% of your interpretation is driven by reading facial expressions and body language.

Transactional Analysis is a large and important field. I introduced it to you here in the hopes you will do a bit of research on your own. It's important to understand TA when trying to understand someone's reaction to your phrasing and gives a tremendous boost to your communication skills.

Remember, this section started out explaining that effective communications were complementary. I explained that your best shot at being understood by your partner requires you to respond from the complementary ego state as your partner and that adult-to-adult communication is the most effective. So what? The "so what" is that when you dig into Transactional Analysis theory and practice you'll realize that mathematically, conversations are more likely to be unsuccessful-to-neutral than successful until you understand how to move someone from child or parent ego state to adult ego state.

The communications deck is stacked steeply against you. The formula is simple: improving your communication skills improves your relationships, whether at work or at home.

Importance of Words

A Thai monk, Achann Chaa of Wat Po Pong, is cited as having created this profound ditty:

> Watch your thoughts, they become words.
> Watch your words, they become actions.
> Watch your actions, they become habits.
> Watch your habits, they become character.
> Watch your character, it becomes your destiny.

Word choice strongly influences not only your ability to communicate complex ideas, but also your ability to steer a conversation toward or away from crisis. Most critically, word choice can do wonders for stopping the implied *blame game*. It also is the key to speaking in adult voice.

If you already use the positive words, then this section will reinforce that. But, if you don't, please consider changing. By the way, these words—and others like them—are important in relationships because the way you *name* events impacts your entire relationship. How you name events also has a strong influence on your outlook on life.

Relationship harmony depends, to some extent, upon agreeing how certain words are used. Here is a brief list of some word pairings that you might find helpful in your relationship(s).

- "Problems" become "challenges"
- "Always" and "never" become "often" and "seldom"
- "Should" becomes "could"
- "Faults" become "differences"
- "Mistakes" become "valuable lessons"

Now to the details:

Changing Specific Words You Use

"Problems" become "challenges:" Speaking negatively, one might say to one's partner: "I'm having a problem with what you just did." From your perspective, this might be both true and accurate; you see what your partner did as a problem. However, words have power and can wound another person inadvertently. In this case, you have labeled the fruits of your partner's work as a "problem," when they, themselves, looked at what they were doing for you as a gift. That is, your partner may have worked very hard at something only now to have their work categorized as a *problem*. Not good on morale. You're also reinforcing in their mind that they are often causing *problems.* Once they start worrying that they represent a "problem" in your life, it is going to set up reactive behavior that makes it even more difficult to get your points across.

In English, *problems* tend to stump someone. They are a blockage, a dead-end. "Problems" carry the connotation of heaviness and negativity. Worse, the word "problem" also carries the implication of blame: the person declaring something a problem is right and the person causing the "problem" is wrong. This is risky speech in a relationship. I urge you not to succumb to the temptation to make your partner fell that they are in the wrong.

The positive way of phrasing might be to say, "This looks like a challenge that we can work through. Let's discuss it tonight after dinner." No emotional loading. Better yet, *challenges* tend to be viewed as temporary—something that you can sit down and puzzle out. It's emotionally lighter, so it is less likely to alarm your partner as you present the issue. Also, by putting the discussion off for an hour or so, you both have time to consider the situation and let your emotions settle down. This approach is the kinder, more gentle approach than calling something a "problem."

"Always" and "never" become "often" and "seldom." A negative statement would be, "You're never ready to leave on time; you always make us late." Very accusatory. The person immediately (and rightfully) becomes massively defensive and starts to shut down emotionally.

An alternative approach could be, "You know, it means a lot to me to be on time to parties, movies, dinner reservations and such. I get stressed and frustrated when we're late. Before we are getting ready to go out next time, I'd like to discuss options so we can leave on time. Will you help me with this?"

One of the problems with extreme words such as *never* and *always* is that they are never true (joke, joke—just checking to make sure you're really following all this). Okay, they are seldom true. Sure, you can say, "The sun always comes up from the east." But this is a scientific comment, not an interpersonal comment. In the soft sciences, very little is absolute. Moreover, extreme words exaggerate the situation and also reveal quite a bit about your own level of mental stress. As absolute words are usually used to criticize a person or situation, the person to whom you're addressing is culture-bound to become **very** defensive. In most cases, the person to whom you're speaking will miss or ignore your message while reeling from your exaggeration.

As the revised approach explains your own feelings and desires, there is no trigger mechanism to invoke defensiveness. You're much more likely to be successful about leaving on time in the future.

"Should" becomes "could." A negative statement (in parent voice) would be, "You should exercise every day and try to stay in shape." An alternate—and more positive—version could be, "Your health is important to me and to us as a couple. Could you tell me how can I support you to develop an exercise routine?"

The first construction shifts all blame/responsibility onto the other person and sets up feelings such as anger, guilt, and shame at not having done what had often been requested. Phrasing the question as a partnership issue opens up possibilities without anger. This also enables the person who gave the directions to examine whether or not their directions were complete, within their partner's skill-set, and that their partner actually understood them and agreed with your approach. Remember The Usual Error: Not everybody thinks as you do.

"Faults" become "differences." "It's your fault you can't find anything in your closet: your closet is a total mess!" Contrast this with, "I'm sorry you keep losing things in the closet. One of the differences between us is that your part of the closet isn't as organized as my side. If you would like, I'll be happy to help you organize your side while I help you find "X."

If you use the word *faults*, you are judging your partner's actions as right or wrong. Your partner is likely to become defensive and resent what you're trying to say to them. Using the word *differences*, removes the critical tone. You're simply pointing out how the two of you process, feel, or act differently. Now, from this point, you can work out methods to handle future situations.

"Mistakes" become "valuable lessons." The negative construction would be, "You made a mistake." The more positive construction would be, "Okay, this didn't work. What can we learn from it?"

The first phrase invites a reaction (and resistance), as your hearer may not at all think they made a mistake. In fact, depending upon their personality, they may actually be driven to find out and present to you how your own request was flawed and how they did the very best they could with the available information which, they go on to point out, was very sketchy and required them to do a lot of unnecessary work even to figure out what they *thought* you wanted.

Not good.

If your partner isn't quite that fast, they may head in the (equally bad) direction of saying to themselves: "Fine, I just won't try this again." As I mentioned earlier, I refer to this as the *Throwing the Baby out with the Bathwater* pattern. Hurt feelings led to a desire to wall off the hurtful experience. The result is a narrowing of your relationship options: the walls are closing in.

Anyway, in these examples, the second (softer) phrasing has you both joined in the problem-solving adventure and enables each of you to learn from the experience. Now, either of you will be more inclined to think expansively about similar situations in the future, once you no longer have to fear accusatory and frightening challenges to your/their ability to think through difficult situations.

The bottom line is that words can be either destructive or constructive. They can tear down or enrich your relationships—whether we're speaking about your relationships with your partner, or relationships with your co-workers.

Now for the hard part; to accomplish this transformation, each of you will need to think before you speak. Your everyday happiness depends upon it.

Beware of One-Word Responses

Not intending to be sexist or politically incorrect, it's been my experience that women seem to put more meaning into single-word responses than do men. This creates fodder for miscommunication.

According to David Cunningham in his article on *Break-Up Busting 101: A Crash Course in Saving a Relationship FAST!*, the three most dangerous words in the English language, with regard to male-female relations, may be **okay**, **fine**, and **sure**, although, he notes, if said by the right woman, "whatever" may take out any one of the other three.

Let's take only a brief look at these words. I'm not going to provide many of Cunningham's examples, because part of your education comes from asking your own partner to give their definitions of these words from the point of view of being involved in an emotional argument.

Male use in non-stressful situations:

- Okay: Not a problem, as in "Okay with me"

- Fine: Of high quality, as in a fine automobile.

- Sure: Affirmative, as in "Sure! I'll be glad to help with that."

- Whatever: Anything, usually used in being agreeable, as in, "Whatever you want is great."

Now, before I mention a few alternate definitions, I want to stress that most women use those words exactly as a man—unless in some kind of emotional argument. Then, the words seem to take on entirely different meanings.

Female use under stressful conditions:

- Okay: "You aren't listening and I am going to shut up now."

- Fine: "You think you know, and I will let you *think* you know, but you know precisely squat about that subject."

- Sure: "It's impossible to communicate with you. You'll never understand."

- Whatever: "I will never speak with you about this again, but I will never forget what you just said."

There's a pattern, here. All of these words have somewhat to very positive meanings for men and for women during normal conversations, but can have a relationship-threatening meaning during angry emotional exchanges.

So, you now have to ask, what happens if you get all four of these *special words* strung together and spat out by that *special kind of woman*? If you ever hear the following sentence:

"Okay, sure, fine! WHATEVER!"

Let me give you a hint. ***Houston, we've got a problem.***

Okay, here's my last shot...

- Relationships that are consciously chosen are usually more rewarding than relationships built on default assumptions.

- Relationships are often different in theory than in practice.

- Being in a relationship that does not meet your needs is not necessarily better than being alone.

- Be flexible.

- Remember: you're supposed to be having fun, that's why you got together (or took this job) in the first place.

Chapter Seven
Some Closing Thoughts

It's easier to live in harmony when you know yourself and the person you're living with. Not "know" as in, "Why, hi, I'm Bob, glad to know you, want to live with me?" But the kind of knowing that builds as you spend quality time together and made an effort to figure out how you and your partner think (process information) and react to a wide range of (often unobvious) challenges.

Most of this book has offered *things to think/talk about* that may not have occurred to you. That's often because we're somewhat blind to the ways we've been brought up; we don't often think about how we think and we don't often challenge our own beliefs. This is one reason we can be so surprised or upset when our partner sees an "obvious solution" to a problem that would never have occurred to us. This is also why it's often very hard to work through or to solve complex issues.

Your relationship can get stressed when your approach to life conflicts with your partner's approach to life. Talking helps, but it can be hard to identify differences between how you and your partner look at the world. Part of the challenge comes from not knowing what you don't know, and part of what you don't know are the motivators underlying your own or your partner's beliefs and actions.

As you move beyond this book and start to work through the reasons for your beliefs and actions, you'll realize how you've been controlled and influenced by your personal upbringing. As you identify these underlying causes, you'll be in the enviable position of being empowered to choose to stay that way or to change. All change will affect your relationship. These changes, themselves, may well improve your relationship(s) to the point that you won't need more heavy-duty problem-solving techniques.

Most of this book is about giving you tools, tips, and techniques for looking at the world (and at your partner) in a new way. Practicing these new techniques will likely change your dynamic in subtle ways.

Closing Statement

This book has been full of ideas. It has presented a new range of communication options. This is both good and bad. It's good, because you now have new ideas to help you to be a great communicator. It's bad because, as Dallin H. Oaks has said: "If we choose the wrong road, we choose the wrong destination."

For many, this book is also either a blessing or a curse. It's a blessing because you now have many new ways to take responsibility for clear communication in your life. It's a curse because you now have nobody to blame for poor communication in your life. As John Burroughs has said: "A man can fail many times, but he isn't a failure until he begins to blame somebody else."

To be in a relationship is to be one of the lucky ones. However, in relationships, luck is the flimsiest currencies of all. Relationships take work. They are dynamic; they change with the wind. When each of you leaves for work in the morning, you're exposed to new ideas. Most of them bounce off you; some of them stick. When you have a lifestyle of coming home and plopping down in front of a television, rather than using the evening to celebrate your partnership and bring interesting and exciting ideas and experiences into your relationship, you're making a choice. When you plop down in front of your television, you're also making a choice not to straighten up the house (or help your partner at some task) and *that*—in and of itself—is a form of communication.

You started your lives as a celebration of your relationship. Now, we suggest that you look at how you relate to one another and consider creating a number of mini-ceremonies to honor the hard work that you've done as you went through this book. You can celebrate where you are now. Honor yourself (and anyone who worked through this book with you) for your commitment to personal improvement on your journey. You may wish to consider writing a Pledge to one another that speaks to your future together.

I certainly thank you for your steadfastness to work through this book, and making it to this page. I always enjoy meeting my readers, so please feel free to come up and say hello.

Robert (Dr. Bob) Rubel
M. Jen Fairfield

Supplementary Material

Preparing for "normal accidents"

Here is a short list to help get you started:

- What happens in a medical emergency?

  - On your cell phone, have you created your ICE list? (In Case of Emergency). Every phone is set up for that. First-responders will immediately check your cell phone for your call list.

  - On your cell phone, are all your medical providers grouped in an obvious way? (On my phone, all doctors are listed with the word "Docs" as their name, then a hyphen, and then the name of the doctor and the specialty.)

  - Do you have a list of your partner's family members and doctors? Do you have a list of their medications? Do you know your partner's wishes about which family members to call first? How about close friends? How about their employer's name and emergency contact number? Do you know the password to your partner's phone and computer?

- Are your legal documents current?

  - Do you and your partner have wills?

- ○ Do you have medical powers of attorney covering such topics as:

  - Resuscitation or not;

  - "No heroic measures;"

  - Mechanical ventilation;

  - Tube feeding;

  - Dialysis;

  - Antibiotics or antiviral medications;

  - Comfort care (palliative care);

  - Organ and tissue donations; and

  - Donating your body.

  - Have you Power of Attorney forms been completed and stored where they can be found easily? Are they on file with your doctor(s)?

- Can anyone find the important details of your life?

  - On your cell phone, consider placing a notepad on your home screen with emergency directions. To make my notepad stand out, my home screen ONLY contains one app: a notepad. There is only one note in that notepad. That note directs the reader to my laptop computer and its password. It further directs the reader how to find a specific file on the root Documents directory that contains detailed instructions about who to contact for various levels of emergency.

- Hint: I suggest that you name the Word file something like: "_ Instructions if I am injured or die." Notice that the first character of the file's name is an underscore mark, then a space. Using an underscore mark forces that file to be the first file listed in that folder.

  ◦ Here are some of the items I list in that Word document:

    - All bank accounts, brokerage accounts along with their passwords. (Note: do not use the actual word "password" or anything like that as a file name or inside a document. Should you lose your computer, you don't want someone to do a global document search for that word.)

    - Location of cash kept in the house (Hint: you can store cash and valuables in a jar in your refrigerator.)

    - List of all bills that are paid directly out of my bank account and the day of the month they come due.

    - List of ongoing services that are not auto drafted.

    - Where I keep my unpaid bills.

- Other special considerations:

  ◦ Are bank accounts joint, so that if one partner is hospitalized the surviving partner can pay current bills?

  ◦ If you have outside investments, what are they and what would someone need to know about them if you are incapacitated for time?

- ◦ Who is listed on the lease or mortgage?

- ◦ Where will the remaining partner live if something happens to the other?

- ◦ What happens if one partner is incapacitated long-term, but doesn't die? Do you have insurance that covers this? Do you have savings to cover basic expenses for a few months?

- Notifications

  - ◦ Who needs to be notified of what facts?

  - ◦ Do family members have Power of Attorney to intercede in financial matters of another family member?

Cited Works

A Russell Hoban Omnibus by Russell Hoban, 1998

Crucial Conversations by Kerry Patterson and Joseph Grenny, 2010

Feeling Good: The New Mood Therapy Revised and Updated by David D. Burns, 2008

Flightdeck Performance: The Human Factor by David O'Hare, 1990

How to Give and Receive Advice by Gerald Nirenberg, 1975

Instant Rapport by Michael Brooks, 1990

Lateral Thinking: Creativity Step by Step Edward DeBono, Reissued 2015

Leadership and Self-Deception: Getting out of the box by The Arbinger Institute, 2010

Men Are from Mars, Women Are from Venus by John Gray, 1992

Modern Man in Search of a Soul by Carl Jung, 1933

Never be Lied to Again: How to get the truth in 5 minutes or less in any conversation or situation by David J. Liberman, 1999

Outliers by Malcolm Gladewll, 2011

Self-Discipline and Emotional Control by Tom Miller (audio CD)

Teaching Thinking Skills: Theory and Practice Joan Boykoff Baron and Robert J. Sternberg, 1986

The Crack in the Cosmic Egg: New Constructs of Mind and Reality by Joseph Chilton Pearce. Revised Edition, 2002

The Godstone and the Blackymor by T. H. White, 1959

The Ideal Problem Solver John D. Bransford and Barry S. Stein, 1993

The Usual Error: Why we don't understand each other and 34 ways to make it better by Pace and Kyeli, 2008

Thinking Better by David Lewis and James Greene, 1985

United Nations Development Programme's "Human Development Report" of July, 2014

Unlimited Power: The New Science Of Personal Achievement by Anthony Robbins, 1997

What Every BODY is Saying: An Ex-FBI Agent's Guide to Speed-Reading People by Joe Navarro and Marvin Karlins, 2008.

What to Say When You Talk to Yourself by Shad Helmstetter, 1990

About the Authors

Robert J. Rubel, PhD
Overview

Dr. Rubel is an educa-
tional sociologist and
researcher by training
and an author, lecturer
and photographer by
choice. For the last
decade, he has written
over a dozen books,
mostly on communica-
tions and relationship

issues of interest to those who live in the world of alternative
sexuality. As a national presenter on things kinky, Dr. Rubel has
presented to over a hundred clubs/events worldwide and (at 71)
continues to present at national conferences 5-8 times a year.

More detail

Bob graduated from the International School of Geneva, in
Geneva Switzerland. He took his undergraduate degree at
Colorado State University in Ft. Collins, Colorado.

Immediately after college he taught high school English for
three years in South-Central Los Angeles. Returning to graduate school, he earned an EdM (Boston University) and PhD
(as a Ford Fellow at the University of Wisconsin, Madison)
in the area educational policy studies with a minor in crim-
inology. After serving a stint as a Visiting Fellow at the U.S.
Department of Justice's National Institute of Justice, he formed
a 501(c)(3) foundation that specialized in crime prevention in

public schools. He ran the National Alliance for Safe Schools for 17 years. During part of that period, he helped create the American Association of Woodturners. For its first three years, Bob served as its Administrator.

Robert has extensive management experience with non-profit organizations and at one point was designated a *Certified Association Executive* through the American Society of Association Executives. He is a heavily published author and has served as founder and managing editor of two national quarterlies, one for school police/security directors, and one for his beloved art-form of woodturning

Mid-career

In his mid-40s, Bob decided to change careers utterly and joined a stock brokerage and future brokerage firm in Washington, D.C. Within six months, he was made a Principal of the futures brokerage side of the firm, and five months after that, was asked to serve as CEO. He ran the company until, four years later, a close friend asked him to return to Austin to help start a new company.

Later years

After five years, Bob retired to pursue his fascination with the world of alternative sexuality, throwing himself into the literature of the field as though it were an academic study. After publishing six books in the 2006-9 period, Bob began lecturing and presenting throughout North America (with brief forays abroad). From 2007-2016, he has presented at nearly a hundred conferences, usually making two or more presentations per event. Most of his topics concern the nearly unending intricacies of communication.

Bob's passion for researching, writing, and lecturing about communication challenges began in 2006 when his then-partner pointed out that he undoubtedly had Asperger Syndrome. Ultimately, a formal psychological evaluation confirmed this strong suspicion. Ever since, he has endeavored to identify and tease apart common communication glitches that can be so destructive in relationships.

Bob, an NLP Practitioner, is an est graduate (1975) and has gone through The Landmark Education Forum two additional times (1997 and 2006) in conjunction with Landmark's 10-week "Communications Workshop."

M. Jen Fairfield

Jen Fairfield is an experienced communicator. She's been forced into this role both as the daughter and wife of military officers, but also in her profession.

Jen has extensive experience managing discussions and interpersonal communications both in her personal and work lives. A master teacher, she created (and taught for five years) a state-certified adult-education course in her professional field. In her work life, Jen has (for over 25 years) been called upon daily to ensure clear (and positive) communication in doctor/patient settings.

Over the past five years, Jen has found her calling attending conferences and workshops, reading books, and working closely
with Dr. Rubel as he has been researching, writing books, and
making presentations both inside and outside the US.

Jen augments Bob's thinking and writing by bringing a fresh
vision. With a 20-year age gap between them, they have very
different views on many subjects. However, she and Bob use
these disagreements as opportunities to explore topics very
differently than either of them would have on our own. They
both grew from these (often contentious) discussions.

Jen has been instrumental in shaping this particular book. She
is responsible for the way the concepts are grouped and flow.
While not NLP-certified, she has had ample exposure to the concepts and principals that she naturally applies to conversations.

Jen has a point-of-view about communication: First, she believes that the cultural connotation of words—more than the
words themselves—fill sentences with the graphic details that
form the basis of one's "social intelligence" (or SI). Second,
she has a backbone of steel and believes that we communicate equally through our actions as through our words. She
believes that *what you do* is *who you are*. She would say: "Your
word is your bond: your honor is based on your word."

Ms Fairfield's eidetic memory has been one the most valuable
gifts she brought to her union with Dr. Rubel. Much to the
benefit of his writing, her memory enables her to assimilate
an amazingly diverse range of ideas on all kinds of topics and
present them with depth and clarity. This book has benefitted
from this ability.

Made in the USA
Monee, IL
03 May 2021